BONEYARD
BADGES

C000124610

BONEYARD BADGES

Aircraft and Emblems at Davis-Monthan AFB

Philip D. Chinnery

Airlife
England

Copyright © 2000 Philip D. Chinnery

First published in the UK in 2000
by Airlife Publishing Ltd

British Library Cataloguing-in-Publication Data
A catalogue record for this book
is available from the British Library

ISBN 1 84037 102 1

The information in this book is true and complete to the best of our knowledge. All recommendations are made without any guarantee on the part of the Publisher, who also disclaims any liability incurred in connection with the use of this data or specific details.

All rights reserved. No part of this book may be reproduced or transmitted in any form or by any means, electronic or mechanical including photocopying, recording or by any information storage and retrieval system, without permission from the Publisher in writing.

Typeset by Rowland Phototypesetting Limited, Bury St Edmunds, Suffolk
Printed in Singapore

Airlife Publishing Ltd
101 Longden Road, Shrewsbury, SY3 9EB, England
E-mail: airlife@airlifebooks.com
Website: www.airlifebooks.com

CONTENTS

INTRODUCTION

The idea came to me following a telephone conversation with a friend who works at AMARC, the Aerospace Maintenance and Regeneration Centre at Davis-Monthan Air Force Base in Tucson, Arizona.

'Hey Phil, you know those B-52s that we scrapped? We removed the panels with the nose art on first. They are going to be sent to the Smithsonian Institute for safe keeping and eventual display.'

A good idea, I thought. So much nose art has been lost over the years, together with squadron badges of units long disbanded and other interesting works of aviation art. Oh to have gone back in time to Kingman Field in 1946 with a good camera and an unlimited supply of the new fangled colour film, just before they started to scrap the 5,000 aircraft they had in storage. Luckily a few samples of nose art were hacked out of the planes before they met their end in the aluminium smelters, hidden in a barn prior to their later discovery and donation to the Confederate Air Force Museum. Again, luckily, a couple of hundred miles away in Tucson Colonel Frank Schirmer, the new boss of the 4105th AAFBU took his camera out to the B-29 storage area and recorded some of the post-World War II nose art before it disappeared forever.

Could I perform a similar role for aviation history, fifty years further on? What kind of artwork is about to disappear at AMARC with the Millennium just around the corner? Why not go and look? A handful of letters and phone calls later I stepped off the Continental jet at Tucson International Airport with my two sons, Mark (18) and Peter (15) to discover that our luggage had gone to Phoenix, two hours' drive away! Mark was just a toddler and Peter was not even born when I first came to the boneyard in 1982. Tucson does not have the tourist attractions of Orlando, Florida, but when I asked them if they would like to spend a week in Arizona they jumped at the chance. I'd tell them about the aeroplanes later. And as for the luggage, Continental redeemed themselves and delivered it to our hotel room that night. I was glad to see it. Walking around Tucson in a three piece suit in 100 degrees of sunshine is as good as carrying a large sign saying 'Englishman'.

To the many British aviation enthusiasts who make the pilgrimage to Tucson I would recommend one or two stops while you are there. Paul Gaudette Books have an enormous stock of military and aviation books in their warehouse at 2050 East 17th Street. Give Paul a ring on 520-791-9412 to make sure he will be there. The Pima Air Museum is also a must. One of the largest aircraft collections in the United States, the museum benefits from its location, AMARC being literally 'just down the road', and many of the exhibits are on loan from there. Transformed out of all recognition since my first visit sixteen years ago, the museum contains over 200 aircraft. Also, news hot off the press from the museum – they have just been awarded the contract to run coach tours of AMARC. Up to now the Air Force have only managed two or three tours each week, but now the museum plans to run them almost hourly during daylight hours. The coach will depart from the museum and further details can be obtained from Bill Davidson, the marketing director at Pima Air and Space Museum. The address is 6000 East Valencia Road, Tucson, Arizona 85706. Phone 520-574-0462, Fax 520-574-9238 or visit their website: www.pimaair.org. Tell them I sent you.

Before I continue the story of my search for aviation artwork in the boneyard, let me stop the story here for a minute. For those readers who have bought my books over the last ten years may I say 'Hi there and welcome back. The story continues so read on.' For the benefit of the new reader who may well have discovered the boneyard for the first time perhaps an introduction to the storage centre would be in order.

The 'Abundance of Strength' badge on this B-52 harks back to the days of colourful SAC wing markings. The motto belongs to the 306th Strategic Wing, which was established in 1948 as a Medium Bombardment Wing.

The boneyard came into being at the end of the Second World War. In May 1945, following the surrender of Nazi Germany the Allied bomber forces in Europe were stood down. Instead of bombs their cargo bays were full of supplies for the starving or prisoners-of-war heading for home. In the Pacific theatre the war continued and plans were being made for a full scale invasion of the Japanese mainland. Back home the aircraft manufacturers continued to produce fleets of bombers in anticipation of the requirement to destroy the Japanese cities and the will to resist of their citizens prior to the landing of the Allies. However, the surprise detonation of atomic bombs over Hiroshima and Nagasaki brought the war to an abrupt end and left the United States Army Air Force with vast numbers of aircraft and nothing to do with them.

Towards the end of 1945 the squadrons of war-weary aircraft began to return home from the far flung corners of the globe. A year after the end of the war almost 34,000 aircraft of all types had arrived at 30 airfields throughout the United States. The majority of them, some 26,700 aircraft, were parked at seven main airfields. The largest number was stored in Oklahoma, at Clinton Naval Air Station. 8,028 Navy aircraft were there, including 1,444 Grumman Wildcats and 1,366 Hellcats. The 5,660 aircraft parked at Walnut Ridge in Arkansas included 87 B-32 Dominator bombers – nearly the entire production run – that were flown direct to Walnut Ridge from the factory at Fort Worth, Texas. Kingman Army Air Field in Arizona held almost as many aircraft as Walnut Ridge with 5,500 aircraft parked nose to tail. About one third of them were B-17 Flying Fortresses, another third were B-24 Liberators; the rest were various types such as the A-20, B-25, B-26, P-38 and P-63. The three other main storage fields were at Altus in Oklahoma (2,543 aircraft), Albuquerque in New Mexico (1,706) and Vernon in Texas (1,322).

With the Germans and British showing them the way, the American aircraft manufacturers turned their attention to the design and manufacture of the new jet engine and many of the aircraft in the armed forces inventory became obsolete overnight. Also, with the end of the war there were just too many aircraft of all types to fulfil the peace-time needs of the United States and the decision was made to scrap or sell to the public the majority of the aircraft in storage. The War Assets Administration and the Reconstruction Finance Corporation were instructed to arrange the disposal of over $9,900,000,000 worth of aircraft. The 'harmless' transport and trainer types of aircraft could be put to good use and sold to the general public, but the fighters and bombers had outlived their usefulness. Soon $8,000,000 worth of aircraft was being scrapped and melted down into metal ingots every day. Rumour has it that the entrepreneur who purchased the aircraft at one of the storage fields recouped his investment just by draining the fuel that was left in the aircraft tanks and selling it.

One exception to the destruction being wrought at the storage fields was Boeing's B-29 Superfortress bomber, the type which had dropped the atomic bombs on Japan. The most modern bomber in the Air Force inventory was to be saved and a war-reserve created, just in case they were needed again. Stalin's armies did not return home after the defeat of Germany; they were now imposing their will on the countries that they occupied, including Poland, Hungary, Czechoslovakia and a large part of Germany. An 'Iron Curtain' was now descending across eastern Europe and the Cold War had begun; our wartime ally was now perceived to be the enemy of the future. Perhaps one day the B-29s would have to carry atomic bombs to targets deep inside the Soviet Union? A handful of air bases in the south-western United States were chosen as storage depots, but their existences were all short-lived except for Davis-Monthan Air Force Base in Arizona, which is still in use today.

The original 640 acres of land on which Davis-Monthan Air Force Base now stands was purchased from the state land department in 1925 for the princely sum of $19.50. The citizens of Tucson named the base in honour of Lieutenants Samuel H. Davis and Oscar Monthan, both Air Corps officers from Tucson. Davis was killed in Florida in 1921 and Monthan died in Honolulu in 1923, both as a result of military accidents. After the Japanese raid on Pearl Harbor the base was expanded and was soon rated as one of the best heavy bombardment training stations in the country. Its location in the Arizona desert made it ideal for all-year-round training and this was taken into account when the search began for a long-term storage airfield for the B-29s and the old cargo workhorse, the C-47.

The main reason for its choice was the climate in the area. The annual rainfall was low, around eleven inches each year, and humidity was low too, between ten and twenty per cent. In addition, the soil, known as 'Caliche' has a low acidic content and is baked so hard by the sun that aircraft can be parked on it, without needing the tarmac or concrete stands which are found at most airfields.

The last Superfortress training unit was deactivated at Davis-Monthan in October 1945 and the base was transferred to the jurisdiction of the San Antonio Air Technical Service Command. The 4105th Army Air Force Base Unit (Air Base) was activated to oversee the new storage depot and by 10 January 1946 the first C-47s and B-29s had arrived. By the end of 1946, 679 B-29s and 241 C-47s were parked in rows, like sleeping soldiers waiting for the call to arms. There were also 30 other aircraft earmarked, with remarkable foresight, for museum preservation. They included the two B-29s *Enola Gay* and *Bockscar* that had dropped the atomic bombs on Japan; the sole XB-19, which until the arrival of the B-36 was the largest aircraft built for the Air Force; the Beechcraft A-38 Destroyer experimental attack plane mounting a 75mm cannon in its long, sharp pointed nose and even a captured German Ju 88.

In 1947 an interesting experiment began, involving the preservation of the B-29s against the harsh desert environment. Known as 'cocooning', the process was performed by the Fort Pitt Packaging Company under 8th Air Force guidelines. Each Superfortress in storage was worth over half a million dollars and to protect them from the sun, wind and sand it was decided to cocoon them in airtight cases. The cocoons would consist of two layers of plastic together with a sealer known as Insulmastic No.4500, a Gilsonite product. It was seven times stronger than rawhide and was designed to keep out dirt and moisture for at least ten years. A contract was awarded to the Fort Pitt Packaging Company to cocoon 486 of the 679 B-29s then in storage and work began in July 1947.

Each of the aircraft was washed and many bags of moisture-absorbing desiccant were placed inside them. The propellers and engine cowlings were covered with masking tape and a first coat of yellow plastic was applied by spray guns to the outside of the aircraft. This was followed by a second, red coat; the colour being changed to ensure that all areas of the aircraft were covered. The black Insulmastic sealer followed and then a final coat of aluminium paint was applied to reflect most of the heat from the sun.

The cocooning project was terminated in May 1948 after 447 B-29s had been treated. Problems soon arose with blisters appearing in the cocoons as trapped air expanded during the heat of the day, breaking the seal of the plastic. Not only that, but when some aircraft were taken out of storage and prepared for return to service, up to 600 man-hours were required to strip the cocoons from each aircraft. It was clear that a better method of preservation was needed for the future.

On 28 August 1948 the designation of the 4105th was changed to the 3040th Aircraft Storage Depot and spare parts removal (reclamation) and salvage was added to the mission of the unit. Forty-seven of the older B-29s and 14 of the museum aircraft were earmarked for spare parts reclamation and with further withdrawals due to East–West tension over the Berlin blockade, the inventory at the end of the year had dropped to 535 B-29s and 187 C-47s. If the figure of 535 B-29s in storage is compared to the 470 then operational with Strategic Air Command

(SAC), the size of the B-29 war reserve at Davis-Monthan Air Force Base can be imagined.

Fortunately for all concerned, the Berlin blockade came to an end in September 1949 without SAC having to go to war. A shortage of C-47 spare parts in the Air Force and the supply of surplus C-47s to various South American governments reduced the number of C-47s in storage by half. The year 1950 also saw two-thirds of the B-29s return to service. The Royal Air Force was in need of a bomber as a stop-gap replacement between the demise of the ageing Lincolns and the arrival of the modern Canberra and V-bomber aircraft. Designated the Washington B Mk 1, 87 B-29s were flown across the Atlantic and served with 9 RAF squadrons until they returned to the desert in 1954.

On 25 June 1950, the North Korean Army crossed the 38th Parallel and invaded South Korea. Within days the lightly armed South Korean Army was in full retreat as town after town was captured by the communist forces. A week later, Strategic Air Command ordered its 22nd and 92nd Bomb Groups to fly to bases in Okinawa and Japan to prepare for conventional bombing missions against the invaders and their supply lines. America was at war again and replacement aircraft would be needed to replace those lost in combat. Two weeks after the start of hostilities, Headquarters Air Materiel Command directed the withdrawal

One of a thousand B-47 Stratojets to arrive for disposal, B-47E 53-6199 was photographed in February 1975 wearing the badge of the 310th Strategic Aerospace Wing. The wing was established in 1952 and deactivated in June 1965.

The 176th Fighter Interceptor Squadron, Wisconsin Air National Guard, retired Convair F-102A Delta Dagger 56-1205 in September 1974. It was converted by Sperry Flight Systems in 1979 as a PQM-102B target drone.

from storage of 50 B-29s for overhaul and reconditioning by the Grand Central Aircraft Company at Tucson Airport.

The Korean War went on for three long years and led to a vast expansion of SAC's bomber fleet. By the end of 1950 the workforce at the 3040th was working flat-out to return stored B-29s to service and to reclaim spare parts from those too old to return to active service. Spare parts worth over $300,000, half the initial purchase price of each aircraft, were being removed from each B-29; these included bombsights, engines, fuel and oil tanks, propellers and instruments. When the aircraft were reduced to stripped-out carcasses they were sold for scrap at $2,300 each.

After each aircraft was stripped of all useable parts the centre of gravity changed drastically and the B-29 would tilt back and sit on its tail. To prevent this, fifteen-feet long, one-foot-square timbers were tied to the nose wheel-well of the aircraft and as many as 25 personnel were loaded into the nose section compartments. The aircraft could then be towed the one and a half miles out to the storage area for 'demilitarisation' prior to sale as scrap. Demilitarisation meant cutting the tail section off the B-29. Heavy cables would be looped over the tail assembly by a crane and attached to a heavy cleat track. The track would take off fast and the cable would contract, slicing the 6,000-pound tail

assembly off and onto a trailer underneath.

By the end of December 1951 only 172 cocooned and 65 non-cocooned B-29s were left in storage. The strength of Strategic Air Command had reached its peak of 540 B-29 bombers, plus 84 RB-29 reconnaissance versions and 256 converted to KB-29 aerial refuelling tankers. Technology was advancing however and the first Boeing B-47 Stratojet bomber had now entered service, joining the other more modern SAC bombers, the B-50 and the B-36 Peacemaker. For the ageing B-29, the writing was on the wall. Having spent the last couple of years returning hundreds of B-29s to service, the 3040th was about to start receiving them all back again. On 1 April 1953, Headquarters Air Materiel Command instructed the storage centre to commence a number of major projects, including processing the arrival of 440 B-29s. In July, as the war in Korea drew to an uneasy close, the first 24 B-29s arrived.

With the signing of the armistice which brought the Korean War to an end, together with the ongoing modernisation of SAC's bomber fleet, the Superfortress was no longer required. The Air Force was now equipping with the giant B-36 Peacemaker and B-47 Stratojet and even the KB-29 aerial refuelling tanker squadrons were now outnumbered twenty to eight by the new KC-

Sikorsky SH-34J Seahorse 148960/3H095 '2E-131' from Navy Helicopter Training Squadron HT-8 was photographed in a bright red paint scheme. It arrived in March 1970 and departed ten years later to Naval Air Engineering Center, Lakehurst, New Jersey.

97 Stratotanker squadrons. As the war-weary bombers began to return to Tucson, other types also started to arrive. By the end of 1953, 120 North American T-6 Texan trainers, 29 Grumman SA-16 Albatross amphibians and 21 Boeing QB-17s had arrived. The QB-17s were Flying Fortresses converted as radio-controlled drones and used as unmanned airborne targets.

With ever-increasing numbers of aircraft arriving for storage, the decision was made to expand the storage area and another 480 acres of land was purchased, increasing the size of the storage centre to 1,290 acres. 1954 was to be the busiest year for the centre since it was established nine years earlier. As the weeks passed, project followed project; aircraft were processed for storage while others were stripped for spare parts and yet others were prepared for departure to other destinations. Confusion reigned however, for no sooner had a project begun than it was changed again. Clearly the project directors at HQ Air Materiel Command and HQ USAF needed to improve their co-ordination and communication. One such example was Project MDA4T of 23 April 1954 which required 57 of the T-6 trainers to be taken out of storage and prepared for departure. The departure schedule was changed four times and in the end only 47 aircraft were required.

Over 30 different projects were started during the year. In February a Navy project was begun involving the dispatch of ten B-29s to the New Mexico Institute of Mining and Technology at Scocorro in New Mexico, for vulnerability tests. 16,830 man-hours were needed to prepare the aircraft and all were dismantled and shipped overland. Parts of these B-29s, including the remains of a former Royal Air Force machine have been discovered at Scocorro in recent years.

In March the first two Boeing B-50 bombers arrived for storage and were due to be followed by 259 others, although the total was soon reduced to 194. By July, work had begun on removing the APS/23 radar sets and APA/44 computers from 77 B-50Ds, and in December the 3040th was instructed to remove 75 more for a one-time flight to Hayes Industries of Birmingham, Alabama, following a decision to convert a number of the B-50s to aerial refuelling tankers.

The destruction of the B-29 fleet began early in the year when work started on reclaiming 183 of those in storage. Their R-3350-23A engines were not needed and remained on the aircraft to be sold as scrap. By the time the last RAF B-29, tail number 44-62259, arrived in September, a further 240 B-29s had been earmarked for salvage. Both the Army and the Navy became involved in the fate of some of the B-29s towards the end of 1954. In August, a 'blast test' project was begun by Army explosive experts from the Aberdeen Proving Grounds in Maryland. Ninety B-29s were used for the tests, which involved the latest developments in explosives. After the explosions, the base fire truck would extinguish any fires and studies would be made to assess the vulnerability and effectual damage to structural areas of the aircraft. In November, a Navy representative from Inyokern, California, arrived to arrange the removal of a number of B-29s by one-time flight to the Navy Proving Grounds at China Lake. Fortunately, some of the China Lake B-29s and a handful that were taken back to the Aberdeen Proving Grounds survived to eventually find their way into various museums.

By June 1954 the inventory of aircraft in storage totalled 1,205 aircraft; 62 SA-16s, 27 B-17s, one B-24 Liberator, one

Junkers 88, 465 B-29s, 120 B-50s, ten L-20s, ten L-23s and 509 T-6s. Soon to arrive were four YC-97 Stratofreighters, although they would be held in temporary storage for departure in the near future. Finally, Strategic Air Command said farewell to the Superfortress when its last B-29A model 42-94032 was retired by the 307th Bomb Wing, arriving at Davis-Monthan on 4 November.

Very little information exists concerning the activities of the 3040th during 1955 and the first half of 1956. It is known however, that the first examples of the Douglas B-26 bomber, Curtiss C-46 Commando and North American F-86 Sabre arrived during that time. Also, 120 of the B-29s were scrapped during the eighteen-month period.

On 1 June 1956 the 3040th Aircraft Storage Squadron (renamed in 1949 from 'depot') at Davis-Monthan Air Force Base was renamed the Arizona Aircraft Storage Branch (AASB). The change of name meant little to the workers at the centre. Their main concern now was how to accelerate the disposal of the 350 B-29s still in storage. The space that they occupied would soon be required for other customers. The first of the giant Convair B-36 Peacemaker bombers was about to arrive.

Left: The Navy Helicopter Combat Support Squadron HC-6 badge is on one of the unit's UH/CH-46A Sea Knights that were retired in 1971 and 1972. Most returned to Navy service a decade later.

Below: The wreckage of this former French Navy Lockheed SP-2H Neptune, 146436, was photographed in the Consolidated Aeronautics scrapyard next to AMARC in 1982. Loaned to the French, it was returned to AMARC in 1973 and sold for scrap in 1976. Note the various 'zaps' on the forward fuselage.

The first Convair B-36 Peacemaker bomber arrived at the Arizona Aircraft Storage Branch (AASB) in the summer of 1956. Ten GRB-36Ds were amongst the first to arrive, followed by the RB-36Ds and RB-36Es of the 99th Strategic Reconnaissance Wing and B-36Ds of the 92nd Bomb Wing. Both units were based at Fairchild Air Force Base, Washington, and ceased B-36 operations between September and November 1956.

A reclamation project began almost immediately to strip certain spare parts from the new arrivals and return them to the Air Force inventory for use on B-36s still in service. Thirty-nine of the aircraft were released to the Mar-Pak Corporation, which was under contract to the Air Force to remove and reclaim certain parts. One year later, with the desert littered with stripped-out carcasses, a smelter was built to melt down the unwanted wrecks.

Around this time, Air Materiel Command instructed the AASB to perform a processing and reclamation test on ten B-36s to determine exactly how many hours were required to reclaim each aircraft. B-36F 49-2681 was the first of the ten to arrive, braking to a halt at the end of the Davis-Monthan runway at 1045 hours on 3 June 1957. All the remaining fuel with the exception of 1,000 gallons was drained and then the aircraft was towed to the industrial area where all loose items were removed, together with the guns and specialised equipment. The remaining fuel and all of the oils were then drained and the aircraft was parked and tied down. The civilian engineers then set to work with their 'save lists' and began removing such items as the propellers and tyres. The desired parts were then cleaned, inspected and sent out to

various storage depots. Sixteen days were required to transform 49-2681 from a front-line strategic bomber into a derelict carcass. The test proved that, although it took 942 man-hours per aircraft and a total cost of $28,930 in labour and materials, the ten aircraft yielded 7,106 spare parts, with a stock value of $7,750,000. With such savings to be made, the AASB was truly in business.

Within a month, the AASB was advised that, due to the planned forthcoming phase-out of the remaining Peacemakers, the requirement for spare parts should rapidly diminish and incoming aircraft were to be placed in temporary storage. The next couple of years saw more work arrive than the storage centre could handle as Air Force Project Streamline IIIR got underway. This ambitious project involved the withdrawal from service of 7,000 aircraft by the end of 1961. Disposal of surplus aircraft took on a new priority and soon three civilian-operated smelters were in action, one owned by Air Associates to dispose of B-29 and B-50 carcasses and the two others, owned by Mar-Pak and Page Airways, were concentrating on the 230 acres of B-36 carcasses. Alongside the contractors' smelters their guillotines were working overtime. These consisted of 8,500 pounds of armour plate dropped from seventy-five feet from the boom of a crane in order to sever parts of the wings and fuselage and cut them into smaller pieces so they could be fed into the smelters.

Foreign military sales were also taking place, with T-28s heading south for the Mexican Air Force; B-26s going to Brazil and T-6s being shipped across the Atlantic Ocean to France. Distribution of excess aircraft to other government agencies and

A field of Lockheed C-121 Super Constellations, including Navy NC-121J 131655 'JB' from Navy Oceanographic Development Squadron VXN-8, which is decorated with Eagle artwork above the nose-wheel door. It arrived in June 1972 and was sold in 1976 to Sun Valley Aviation of Phoenix.

Douglas EA-1F Skyraider 132437 was wearing the badge of Navy Attack Squadron VA-122 above the 'NJ' on its fin when photographed in February 1975. The Skyraider made a name for itself in Vietnam in the Search-and-Rescue support role due to the amount of time it could spend in the air and the weight of ordnance it could carry.

other branches of the military, or donations to eligible organisations, was now an alternative to automatic disposal in the furnaces of the smelters.

The peak of the Streamline IIIR aircraft phase-out took place during 1959 and 1960. In the twelve months to June 1959, 652 more aircraft arrived, including the 432nd and last B-36 and 43 B-47 Stratojet bombers. Amongst the aircraft movements was the arrival of B-29 45-21800 which had been modified to carry Chuck Yeager's experimental Bell X-1 aloft, and the departure of B-36J 52-2220, which made the last Peacemaker flight on 29 April 1959 when it flew out of Davis-Monthan to the site of the new Air Force Museum at Wright-Patterson Air Force Base in Ohio.

On 1 August 1959 the Arizona Aircraft Storage Branch was redesignated the 2704th Air Force Aircraft Storage and Disposition Group (AFASDG) and began to report directly to HQ, Air Materiel Command. In the same month, 110 C-46 cargo aircraft and 94 B-26 bombers went on sale. As the Air Force squadrons continued to disband, 500 more North American F-86 Sabres arrived, together with the first examples of the Century Series of fighters; the F-100 Super Sabre, F-101 Voodoo, F-104 Starfighter and F-105 Thunderchief. The first B-57 Canberra and B-66 Destroyer bombers arrived and the number of B-47 Stratojets being retired also increased as Boeing's new B-52 Stratofortress came into service.

Almost 2,000 more arrivals brought the June 1960 inventory up to over 4,000 aircraft, despite 1,000 more aircraft being scrapped in the meantime. These included 375 F-84s which were, at one time, stacked three or four high awaiting disposal. The last WB-29 Weather Service aircraft were retired in 1960 and were the last B-29s sent to Davis-Monthan for disposal. The

Boeing B-29 Superfortress, which had first flown in 1942, had at last reached the end of the line. Today, of the 3,960 B-29s produced, less than three dozen still survive, including 44-86292 *Enola Gay*, immortalised as the aircraft that dropped the first atomic bomb on Hiroshima on 6 August 1945. The bomb, dubbed 'Little Boy' contained the power of 20,000 tons of TNT and destroyed 4.7 square miles of the city, killing or injuring 140,000 people. Another B-29 to escape the smelter was *Bockscar* which dropped the second atomic bomb, 'Fat Man', on Nagasaki on 9 August 1945. The casualties and damage, although fewer and less than at Hiroshima, coupled with the Soviet Union's declaration of war on Japan the previous day and the months of B-29 attacks on Japanese cities, finally convinced the Japanese to surrender unconditionally.

The last B-36 sale took place in May 1960 and included all remaining Peacemakers. The magnitude of the disposal programme taking place can be imagined when one realises that this last B-36 carcass sale amounted to 2,800 tons of scrap metal and the lot was sold for over half a million dollars. The last carcass had been smelted by 2 October 1961 and the once mighty Peacemaker fleet ceased to exist. When the dust had settled and the furnaces had cooled, only five B-36s remained, preserved at various air bases.

Headquarters, Air Materiel Command was now aware of the potential value of its Davis-Monthan storage centre; over one twelve-month period, $64 million worth of spare parts had been returned to Air Force stocks. As a result, they authorised the construction of a new industrial complex and an increase in staff to 737 civilians and fourteen military personnel. Half a million dollars was spent on a new reclamation building with a 918-feet-

'Flying Bucket of Bolts' artwork is visible on the wreckage of a Bell UH-1 Huey believed to be UH-1A 58-2080 which was retired in 1971. It was photographed in the Allied Aircraft scrapyard just outside AMARC in January 1982.

long roof, which not only protected the workers from the desert sun but provided 180,000 square feet of shelter to house the reclamation processing, packaging, crating and shipping functions.

The new reclamation shelter changed the entire pattern of routine reclamation. Aircraft could now be towed to the shelter and workers would carry out their tasks under its shade instead of in the open at the mercy of the burning sun. No longer would all reclaimed parts jolt around in the back of a truck for up to a mile between the aircraft from which they had been removed and the location where cleaning, sorting and other steps prior to shipment took place.

In April 1961, Air Materiel Command was divided into two parts; the Air Force Systems Command and the Air Force Logistics Command. The 2704th now reported directly to HQ AFLC. By this time, 300 more B-47 Stratojets had arrived and six more Bomb Wings were scheduled for deactivation.

In the summer of 1961, strained relations between the United States and the Soviet Union over Berlin led to the decision to postpone the planned deactivation of six Bomb Wings of B-47s and six air refuelling squadrons of KC-97 tankers. The discovery by an SAC U-2 spyplane of Soviet ballistic missiles being installed in Cuba in October resulted in President Kennedy placing Strategic Air Command on full alert, and the 2704th halted all B-47 spare part reclamation and prepared to return a large number to service if required. Fortunately the crisis passed when Russia backed down and with the imminent delivery of the last B-52 and B-58 Hustler bombers, the retirement of the remaining B-47s could begin in earnest. The 2704th was ready for the influx of Stratojets; it had now expanded to 1,744 acres and with a mere 2,700 aircraft in storage in June 1963 it had plenty of room to spare.

In 1964 yet another money-saving proposal by the Department of Defense led to the closure of the Navy aircraft storage centre at Litchfield Park near Phoenix, 150 miles north of Davis-Monthan. Its function was to be combined with that of the 2704th as a single manager operation and to reflect its new multi-

service role the centre was redesignated on 1st February 1965 the Military Aircraft Storage and Disposition Centre (MASDC). The mission of the renamed centre was defined as 'the processing and maintaining of aircraft in storage; preparation of aircraft for one-time flight or transfer; reclamation of aircraft/aircraft engines and components for inventory replenishment and/or special projects; processing of aircraft/aircraft engines and residue for disposal; administration of sales and/or service contracts with foreign governments, other government agencies and commercial contractors.'

To ensure that their interests would be taken care of, the Navy opened a Field Service Office at MASDC and the transfer of 800 aircraft from Litchfield Park began. Five hundred of them were moved by truck, because of the cost involved to strip away each aircraft's preservative and prepare it for a 150-mile flight to MASDC. It cost $350 per aircraft and saved more than a million dollars. A further 1,000 acres were added to the centre, making a total of 2,729 acres, and this more than accommodated the 2,000 Air Force and 800 Navy aircraft and the first early-model B-52 bombers which began to arrive in May 1965.

The United States was now involved in a 'shooting war' in South-east Asia and the search was on for a suitable counter-insurgency aircraft that could fly low and slow and carry a heavy bomb load. The spotlight fell on MASDC and soon nearly 400 surplus Navy A-1 Skyraiders were being prepared for further service. They were joined by Air Force B-26 bombers and T-28 Trojan trainers which were withdrawn from storage and sent to overhaul depots where they would be modified for their new ground-attack role. In addition, the planned expansion of the South Vietnamese Air Force led to the transfer of C-47s, A-1s and T-28s to the new battlefields of Vietnam and Laos.

A use was found for the lines of vintage C-47 'Gooney Bird' transports sitting in the desert. The Air Force withdrew 33 from storage, fitted them with three 7.62mm mini-guns in the port windows and cargo door and sent them to Vietnam. With each gun capable of firing 6,000 rounds per minute, the AC-47 gunships were flown by Air Commando Squadrons to protect Special Forces camps and isolated outposts. Known by their callsign 'Spooky', they were also dubbed 'Puff, the Magic Dragon' by those who had witnessed the streams of tracer bullets pouring through the darkness towards the ground, as the aircraft flew a left-hand pylon turn around the target.

As the war escalated and the Air Force began to fly bombing missions into North Vietnam, seven RB-66B Destroyers were dispatched from MASDC to join those already operating from bases in Thailand and South Vietnam. The B-52 bombers based on Guam were now flying daily 'Arc Light' missions against the Viet Cong and the wear and tear on their engines led to a request to MASDC for two dozen J57-29 power packs, to be removed from B-52Bs in storage. In the twelve months to June 1966, MASDC shipped 51,000 spare parts and engines to support the war effort.

Between 1945 and 1966, 14,000 aircraft had arrived at Davis-Monthan and only 2,800 had flown out again. Very few aircraft of World War II vintage were now left at MASDC. One of the last, a DB-17P Drone Director aircraft, departed on a five-year lease to the International Flight and Space Museum in Ontario, California. Ironically, Ontario received 2,000 surplus aircraft at the end of the war and the majority, including B-17s were scrapped.

On 28 June 1966 MASDC received a new far-sighted and imaginative commander, Colonel I.R. Perkin. He immediately set to work improving the image of the storage centre. With the aim of publicising the work of MASDC and its value to the taxpayer, a brochure and twenty-minute film were produced, appropriately titled *Desert Bonanza*. The new commander also authorised a display of a number of museum-type stored aircraft along the perimeter fence where they could be seen by the public. This was the forerunner of today's 'Celebrity Row'. He was also the driving force behind the idea of founding an air museum in Tucson.

Eventually a site was chosen for the Pima Air Museum and the 35 aircraft on display at the base were moved there. The collection has now grown to over 200 aircraft and the museum receives around 150,000 visitors each year. A unique arrangement with the storage centre allows the museum to display aircraft on loan from 'across the road' and has guaranteed a good supply of exhibits for the foreseeable future.

Inter-service transfers were now becoming commonplace and one such agreement involved the transfer of 28 Navy EC-121 airborne early warning aircraft to the Air Force for use in South-east Asia. The Air Force was also in dire need of replacement engines for its bombers, so 266 B-52 and B-66 engines were shipped out. By now the 60 early-model B-52s in storage had been virtually picked clean and within a year all would have been scrapped.

The Air Force was also retiring large numbers of reciprocating-engined cargo and transport aircraft such as the C-117, C-118 and T-29. The cost and scarcity of high octane fuel contributed to their replacement by jet-engined aircraft. A large number of the T-29s would eventually find their way on to the civilian aircraft market. Another type affected was the C-124 Globemaster II fleet, which was also suffering from wing defects. All but a handful of these huge transports had their engines removed and were later broken up.

The Navy had now retired its A-1E Skyraiders and 53 were transferred to the Air Force for use by the Special Operations Squadrons (formerly Air Commando Squadrons) flying close air support and search-and-rescue missions over Laos and South Vietnam. A very tough aircraft, the Skyraider was ideal for the role and four Air Force squadrons flew the type in South-east Asia.

In 1968 some of the older types of aircraft began to return to MASDC from the South Vietnamese Air Force. These were C-

Navy Lockheed DP-2E Neptune 128347/1P399 was used as a drone-control aircraft by Composite Squadron VC-5 until its retirement in May 1976. It was sold in 1985 to Air Met Corporation of Tucson.

47D transports and H-34 helicopters and one or two were still to be found at Davis-Monthan in the mid-1980s. Norway had already returned three dozen F-86 Sabres loaned to them under the Military Assistance Programme and these were now joined by seven C-119G transports, all of which would be broken up and scrapped. The Army had begun to use MASDC shortly after the Navy moved in from Litchfield Park; now the Coast Guard appeared on the scene, retiring the first two of their HU-16 Albatross amphibians.

The 1969 inventory stood at 3,576 aircraft and helicopters. Approximately 67 per cent were in storage, 15 per cent were awaiting reclamation, 10 per cent were hulks awaiting sale for scrap and 7 per cent were of the Reclamation Insurance Type (RIT) status. This latter category applied to certain aircraft set aside as a source of spare parts, to keep active aircraft flying. Reclamation of the 1,000 B-47 Stratojets retired by Strategic Air Command had begun in December 1967 and by June 1969 over 300 had been scrapped. Eventually the whole fleet would be sold for scrap to Allied Aircraft Sales of Tucson.

Strategic Air Command began to retire their two B-58 Hustler Bomb Wings in November 1969 and within three months all 84 were in storage. A couple were earmarked for museums, but the rest were sold to Southwestern Alloys in 1977 and broken up for scrap. Metal fatigue was also plaguing the C-133 Cargomaster fleet, which had been in service since 1957 and was often used to transport Atlas, Thor and Jupiter missiles. The fifty-strong fleet was purchased in 1973 by Allied Aircraft Sales and Kolar

Incorporated, who sold a handful as potentially flyable and fed the rest into their smelters. The pollution caused by smelters led the Pima County Air Pollution Control Department to complain about their use, and as a result contractors were now required to remove all aircraft carcasses to off-base smelters, where they would come under the jurisdiction of pollution control officials.

In accordance with President Richard Nixon's policy of 'Vietnamisation' the United States had begun to withdraw from South-east Asia and was attempting to build up the Air Forces of the countries under threat from the North Vietnamese. Four dozen C-123 Providers were shipped to South Vietnam, including 16 from MASDC and 10 UH-34G helicopters left for Laos to be used by Air America, the clandestine airline run by the Central Intelligence Agency to support the anti-communist forces in the country.

The American expertise in converting aircraft to gunships was used to produce 13 AU-23A gunship versions of the Pilatus Turbo-Porter, which were sent to Thailand from MASDC for counter-insurgency operations. Fourteen AU-24A Helio Courier gunships were sent to Cambodia where they were used with great success against the Khmer Rouge.

With the winding-down of the war in South-east Asia MASDC received notification of Operations Plan 'Pacer Harvest', which provided guidance for the expected arrival of aircraft after the American withdrawal. Amongst the first aircraft to arrive were AP-2 and NC-123 gunships. The 3 AP-2H Neptunes were from Navy Heavy Attack Squadron VAH-21, based at Cam Rahn Bay,

The lumps and bumps on this Convair Samaritan identify it as EC-131G 141024 which was used by the Pacific Missile Test Centre until its retirement in November 1979. It was sold in March 1985 to Hamilton Aviation of Tucson.

The 111th Fighter Interceptor Training Squadron, Texas Air National Guard, retired their F-101F Voodoos in July and August 1982. 57-0342/FF418 was one of the last of the type to arrive. It departed for Charleston Air Force Base, South Carolina, in 1988. The unit later equipped with the F-4 followed by the F-16.

from where they had flown over 200 missions using their guns and bombs on enemy road and river traffic in the Mekong Delta. Two 'Black Spot' NC-123K Providers also arrived for removal of classified equipment, used in testing new systems for future designs of gunships. They were then passed on to the Thai Air Force who were in need of transport aircraft.

By June 1971 the total number of aircraft in storage had risen to 4,605, including 400 TH-55A training helicopters from the recently closed Army helicopter training establishment at Fort Wolters in Texas. The B-47 fleet had now been reduced to 56 aircraft and reclamation had begun on 200 F-102 Delta Daggers. The end of 1971 saw the centre covered by five inches of snow, an unusual and unexpected occurrence. It remained for a whole day

before the desert sun got the better of it. A request for a hard surface work ramp in the industrial area for the preparation of aircraft for flight was turned down due to the estimated cost of three million dollars. However, MASDC was made the distribution centre for the AM-2 matting that had been used in Vietnam for temporary airfields. Four hundred truck loads provided the centre with a 183,000 square-yard apron, the largest in the world at that time.

In the twelve months to June 1973, 2,130 more aircraft had arrived for storage, bringing the total to an all-time high of 6,080 aircraft and missiles. Approximately 2,500 belonged to the Air Force, 1,900 to the Navy, 1,500 to the Army and 6 belonged to the Coast Guard.

Although South Vietnam was not finally defeated by the North Vietnamese communists until 1975, the United States' involvement came to an end in January 1973. Many aircraft were left behind for the South Vietnamese Air Force, but the majority returned to the United States, many destined for retirement. With 6,080 aircraft in storage at MASDC in 1973 the problem facing the Department of Defense planners was, what to do with them all?

One suggestion involved the replacement of the Air Force's sub-scale Firebee One and Two aerial targets with life-size surplus aircraft. The F-102 Delta Dagger possessed a marked silhouette likeness to the enemy Su-19, MiG-19 and MiG-25, and they were available off-the-shelf from MASDC. The Air Force awarded a contract to the Sperry Corporation in 1973, to convert 215 F-102s into remote-controlled target drones. The rebuild programme was called 'Pave Deuce' and the F-102s were taken out

of storage and ferried to the Sperry Corporation facility at Crestview, Florida, and from 1978 onwards, to their Litchfield Park factory near Phoenix. They were then stripped and modified to fly by remote control, to end their days as flying targets in the skies over missile ranges in the New Mexico desert and over the Gulf of Mexico.

The vast increase in the Army helicopter inventory, as a result of the Vietnam War, meant that they could now dispose of some of the older types of helicopter in storage at MASDC. Consequently, 1974 saw the first sale of some of the 500 H-13 Sioux and 400 H-23 Raven training and observation helicopters. A large number were sold to civilian owners and many more were supplied to various state agencies such as Forestry Departments, Civil Defense units, Police Departments and, for instruction purposes, to technical colleges and schools.

A ferocious sea dragon is the main feature of Tactical Electronic Warfare Squadron VAQ-130's badge found on one of their EKA-3Bs in the RIT area in 1988. It has since been sold for scrap. The squadron became the first operator of the EA-6B Prowler.

The Navy had 300 trainer versions of the F-9 Cougar carrier-based fighter in storage. The type had first flown in 1951 and was now obsolete. Southwestern Alloys purchased the first 100 offered for sale as scrap in 1974 and Sun Valley Aviation bought the remainder two years later. The Navy also had over 100 T-1 Sea Star deck-landing trainers that were now obsolete. They went on sale in the summer of 1974 and were all purchased for scrap by Allied Aircraft Sales of Tucson.

To prevent combat-type aircraft falling into the wrong hands, they have to be demilitarised prior to removal from the centre. This process simply requires the purchaser to cut the wings and tail assembly off, thus rendering future reassembly and flight impossible. Generally speaking, transport aircraft and helicopters can be sold intact and can therefore command a higher price. They have usually been subjected to spare parts reclamation though, and need careful restoration before certification by the FAA. One such type was the C-54 Skymaster, the military version of the four-engined DC-4 commercial transport aircraft. The first of 80 went on sale in 1974, with many being purchased for conversion to fire-fighting water bombers.

Aircraft still arrived for storage, although in fewer numbers than before. One interesting type which arrived was the WB-57F Canberra, 8 having been sent into retirement following the disbandment of the 58th Weather Reconnaissance Squadron on 1 July 1974. They had been greatly modified with new wings spanning 122-feet, twice the normal size, and 2 huge TF-33 turbofan engines. They were used for very high altitude reconnaissance and air sampling duties and a NASA example is currently on display at the Pima Air Museum.

The last two C-124 Globemaster IIs also arrived during the year from the Georgia Air National Guard. One of them left in August 1975 for the USAF Museum and the rest of the fleet, minus their engines and undercarriages, was sold in 1976 for scrap. The second of the pair also escaped the axe and was sold to a civilian buyer, who flew it to Las Vegas, Nevada, where it was painted blue and white. It has remained there ever since. Another transport type which began its retirement in 1974 was the Convair T-29 and 86 of them arrived during that year. They continued to arrive until the end of 1975, by which time there were 300 of them in storage. The following year the sales of the type began and many found their way on to the civil market. The Air National Guard also retired its last 50 F-100C Super Sabres during 1974. At the end of 1975 the first of 350 'D' and 'F' models would begin to arrive, earmarked to follow in the footsteps of the last F-102s.

The year 1975 saw the final collapse of South Vietnam, but not before over 120 South Vietnamese Air Force aircraft had flown out to Thailand. These included 25 A-37B Dragonfly ground attack aircraft, which were sent to MASDC in June and July. Fourteen C-130 Hercules transports had also escaped to Thailand and Singapore and four of these also arrived at MASDC in 1976. Almost 70 USAF C-118 Liftmasters were retired to MASDC in 1975. Most of them were sold the next year to civilian operators, although a few were transferred to the Navy. The Liftmaster was the first Military Airlift Command aircraft to fly the Atlantic non-stop. In 1964 they were assigned to MAC aeromedical evacuation units in the United States. They were used in Europe and the Pacific, including Vietnam, for evacuation of patients from combat areas and from theatre points of pickup. Their replacement is the jet-equipped C-9 Nightingale, the military version of the DC-9 airliner.

The last C-119 'Flying Boxcars' were retired by the Air Force and Marine Corps in 1975. The majority had been sold for scrap by 1979, although five remained in the RIT area until their hulks were sold in April 1990. Many C-119Gs were converted to AC-119G Shadow and AC-119K Stinger gunships and flown in combat in Vietnam. (Readers in the United States might like to read the author's book *Air Commando*, published by St Martins Press of New York, for the story of the Shadows and Stingers service in Vietnam.)

The Navy's A-6B Intruder first appeared at MASDC in July 1975, when two were processed in from Attack Squadron 34. They remained in storage for three years until they were flown out for conversion to A-6Es and eventual return to service. As of the publication date of this book, the last A-6 has now finally been retired to the desert.

Surplus Air Force and Army utility aircraft were offered for sale in large numbers from 1975 onwards and nearly all took up civilian registrations. These included 50 short take-off and landing (STOL) U-10 Couriers, a favourite of the CIA in South-east Asia, and 200 U-6A Beavers.

Supplies of aircraft to friendly governments continued during 1975 and a score of T-33s and 6 F-104s were withdrawn from storage and flown to Taiwan to join the Chinese Nationalist Air Force. This continued into 1976, when the 27 A-37B Dragonflies that had survived the fall of South Vietnam were supplied to South Korea. They were supplemented in 1977 by 6 C-123 Provider transport aircraft, retired earlier by the Alaskan Air National Guard.

Several large aircraft sales took place in 1976, consisting mainly of reclaimed fighters and bombers. The Navy no longer had any use for its TF-8A Crusader training aircraft and Consolidated Aeronautics, a local scrapyard, purchased 50 of them. The Sun Valley Aviation Company of Phoenix purchased 150 Navy TF-9 Cougar fighters and 25 EB-66 Destroyer aircraft. The latter were light tactical bombers, modified by the Air Force and used extensively over North Vietnam by their Electronic Warfare Squadrons. The film *Bat-21* detailed the rescue of a crew member from a shot down EB-66 at the height of the North Vietnamese invasion of the South at Easter 1972.

Sun Valley Aviation also purchased a handful of derelict F-102s in 1976 and obtained 100 more in 1977. The B-58 Hustler bombers which had been in storage since 1970 also came under the hammer in 1977 and all 82 were purchased by Southwestern Alloys. They were towed across to their yard just outside the perimeter fence of MASDC, broken up and melted down into ingots in their furnace.

Sixty HH-43F Huskie helicopters were purchased by Allied Aircraft in 1977. It was the first helicopter used by the Air Force especially for airborne fire-fighting and crash rescue operations. Allied had also bought two dozen OH-43D Marine Corps versions five years earlier. Two helicopters, one of each version, are currently on display at the nearby Pima Air Museum. The year 1977 also saw an upgrading of the centre's processes for examining reclaimed parts. It is necessary to be able to determine which spare parts are serviceable for re-use from among those that are damaged or worn out. The two inspection processes then in use were a liquid penetrant test and a magnetic particle inspection. The liquid penetrant examination of aircraft parts was carried out by placing the part in a dye bath, which would reveal cracks inside the item when the part was exposed to a black light. This process was used for parts composed of aluminium, stainless steel and other materials which cannot be magnetised. Parts composed of metals which could be magnetised were subjected to magnetic particle inspection. The part to be inspected would be coated with powdered steel shavings mixed with kerosene and when it was exposed to black light the cracks would show up as lines.

Three new processes were then introduced; X-ray inspection, ultrasonic inspection and eddy current inspection. The X-ray machine used to inspect aircraft parts was much more powerful, at 150,000 volts, than medical machines. In the ultrasonic inspection, fluid was put on the part and high frequency sound waves sent through the item registered pulses on a scope, to indicate whether or not there was a flaw in it. Lastly, the eddy current technique was used by measuring the pattern of flow of an electric current thrust into the part.

By the end of 1977, 1,424 aircraft were awaiting reclamation, the largest number being 171 Navy T-33s; 523 aircraft were awaiting sale, transfer or donation to appropriate agencies and 2,355 aircraft and helicopters were in storage. Times had changed, though, and the majority of the stored aircraft – 1,108 – belonged to the Navy, with 678 belonging to the Air Force, 563 to the Army and 6 to the Coast Guard. Amongst the Navy aircraft to arrive in 1977 were 7 S-3A Vikings. The S-3 was taking over the anti-submarine search and strike role from the S-2 Tracker, and 161 of the latter were in long-term storage, with another 116 undergoing reclamation at the end of the year.

In 1978 Strategic Air Command retired 60 of its older B-52D and F models to MASDC. At the same time the Texas Air National Guard retired the last KC-97L Stratotankers from service. Over 600 C-97s had been retired to MASDC over the years. They have proved surprisingly popular in the aircraft sales, despite the government requirement that the purchaser must remove the refuelling boom and pumps from the fuel tanker versions.

Helicopter sales resumed in 1978 with the first of 300 obsolete TH-55A trainers being put out to tender. Foreign military sales also continued with 35 F-8H Crusaders going to the Philippine Air Force. One of the more interesting types of aircraft to arrive in 1979 was the EB-57E Canberra, retired by the 17th Defense Systems Evaluation Squadron at Malmstrom AFB, Montana. They were equipped with the latest devices for jamming and penetrating air defences and were used to simulate an enemy bomber force attempting to find gaps in the air defence systems. The final examples of the EB-57 were retired by the 134th DSES, Vermont Air National Guard in 1982.

Boeing and McDonnell Douglas both fielded two prototype aircraft for the Advanced Medium STOL Transport (AMST) competition in the early 1970s. Both types underwent testing and evaluation at Edwards AFB by the manufacturers and Air Force Systems Command officials. The programme was suspended in 1979 following the withdrawal of Air Force funding, and the two McDonnell Douglas YC-15As arrived at MASDC in August 1979, followed by the two Boeing YC-14As in April 1980. One of each type has been loaned to the Pima Air Museum on the condition that they be returned at 24 hours notice if required.

The Air Force Reserve began to retire its C-123K Providers in June 1980 and some have since appeared on the civil market, in the colours of one of the fire-bomber companies. Two or three others have been withdrawn from storage, allegedly for use by certain government agencies for tasks involving clandestine flights to South American countries. Examples have even been

Liberally covered in graffiti, Navy Lockheed EC-130Q Hercules 156172 arrived in June 1990 and was scrapped in September 1997. It was last used by Fleet Air Reconnaissance Squadron VQ-4 at NAS Patuxent River, Maryland, which replaced the type with the Boeing E-6A for communications support of Fleet ballistic missile submarines.

seized by the Drugs Enforcement Agency; apparently the type has potential for use by drug runners. At the time of the author's most recent visit the remainder of those still in storage had been moved to an isolated area as a result of concern over their use in Vietnam to spray the infamous Agent Orange defoliant.

The phase-out of the F-105 Thunderchief also began in the summer of 1980 when the 35th Tactical Fighter Wing at George AFB, California, replaced its F-105F Wild Weasels with the F-4G. There were still a couple of years to go before the last would retire, having given stalwart service for over two decades, including the years of war in South-east Asia from which 397 of them did not return.

Visitors to MASDC in September 1981 had to blink and look again at the sight of 17 American Airlines Boeing 707s on the arrival ramp. They were the first of over 130 civilian Boeing 707s purchased by the Air Force, including the bulk of the Trans World Airlines fleet. All were being preserved in storage, after the removal of their engines and vertical and horizontal stabilisers, for future use by the KC-135 tanker fleet. The commercial carriers could no longer operate the Boeing 707s economically and the Air Force bought them for between $500,000 and $1 million each. Spare parts worth many times that have been removed from each aircraft.

On 12 January 1982 the first F-106A Delta Dart arrived for storage from the 48th Fighter Interceptor Squadron. Over 100 had arrived by December 1985 when it was announced that, under an Air Force programme called 'Pacer Six' about 200 F-106s would be converted to drones and used as aerial targets by the Air Force and Army. The Air Force began replacing the F-106s with the F-15 Eagle and earmarked the Delta Dart as a replacement for the PQM-102 and QF-100 drones. Tactical Air Command planned to use the new drones until 1995 and then replace them with F-4 Phantom drones, following that type's retirement from service.

As a follow-on to the 'Pave Deuce' F-102 drone conversion programme, Sperry's Defense and Space Systems Division began converting the first of 80 F-100 Super Sabres to QF-100 drones in 1983. In addition, Flight Systems Incorporated at Mojave, California, commenced the conversion of 209 more.

Sales of Navy aircraft began to take off with 80 S-2 Trackers and 48 E-1 Tracers – the latter an airborne early warning version of the S-2, being sold to Consolidated Aeronautics of Tucson. Although all had suffered spare parts reclamation, they were offered for sale as potentially flyable and many are still stored by the company in Tucson. Despite the fact that one or two S-2s have been acquired by warbird enthusiasts, the main commercial market for them is fire-bomber operators, a large number being supplied to the California Division of Forestry and their counterparts in Canada and France. A number of South American countries were also interested in MASDC's stocks of surplus S-2s and in 1981 Grumman overhauled and supplied Trackers to Brazil and then in 1982 to Uruguay.

Douglas A-4 Skyhawk stocks at MASDC were reduced by around 100 in 1983. Allied Aircraft won a contract to crate and ship 16 TA-4Bs to Singapore, who had received an initial batch of A-4Cs in 1980. Eighty-eight more were removed to an overhaul facility where 40 complete examples were to be made for the Air Force of Malaysia. The summer of 1983 also saw 15 ex-Navy F-4J Phantoms fly out for overhaul, prior to despatch to England to add another Phantom squadron to the Royal Air Force. This reinforced the RAF Phantom strength, spread thin by the need to maintain a squadron at operational readiness on the Falkland Islands.

Portugal was next on the list to receive surplus Navy aircraft. Thirty A-7s were crated and sent to the Vought Corporation's factory in Dallas for modification into 24 A-7Ps and 6 TA-7Ps. As fast as the Navy reduced their inventory at MASDC,

more aircraft arrived to increase it again. From 1983 onwards more A-7s were retired, together with over 250 Navy and Marine Phantoms. Over two dozen early model P-3A Orion patrol aircraft arrived for storage. Some were earmarked for transfer to the Customs Service, while reclamation soon began on others. Eventually, Foreign Military Sales would see the departure of others to friendly nations.

The Air Force had also been busy and 40 B-52s were sold for scrap, leaving around 230 others still in storage. As a part of the Strategic Arms Reduction Treaty (START) the B-52s have to be dismembered and left for 120 days so that Soviet satellites can verify their destruction.

In 1984 the Air Force also found a use for two of the DC-130 Hercules transports which had been used to launch remote-controlled drones in Vietnam and were retired in 1979. The Aeronautical Systems Divisions 4950th Test Wing at Wright-Patterson AFB requested them for use as testbed aircraft for new electronic components. The idea saved the Air Force about $28 million, the basic price of two new C-130s.

Over the decade following the United States' withdrawal from South-east Asia, the wheel had turned full circle. The old obsolete types had largely gone and those that were left were proving their worth as spare parts 'banks'. The numbers of aircraft arriving for storage were slowing down due to a trend in the armed forces of retaining their aircraft longer. New aircraft are expensive to build and repair, so the spare parts bank at MASDC had become more valuable. The success of the centre was reflected in its balance sheets. For every dollar spent on its upkeep in 1984, MASDC was able to return $13.18 to the government.

Surfer artwork can be seen on the tail of Navy EC-130Q Hercules 156173, which was retired by Navy Fleet Air Reconnaissance Squadron VQ-4 in May 1990 and scrapped in September 1997.

The Air Force decided to change MASDC's 'aircraft boneyard' image in 1985 and renamed the centre the Aerospace Maintenance and Regeneration Center (AMARC). This change also reflected an addition to the workload of the centre with the development of an aircraft contingency withdrawal programme. This was designed to supply the armed forces in a national emergency with mission-capable aircraft on short notice.

During the fiscal year 1985 $301 million worth of spare parts were returned to military warehouses, an increase of 74 per cent over FY84, and 173 aircraft were reclaimed for spare parts, an increase of 49 per cent over the previous year. Because of the increased re-utilisation of parts and aircraft, particularly in the form of target drones, the financial return to the government doubled to $26.54 for each dollar spent.

In late September 1985 one aircraft burst into life after nine years in storage when a Lockheed EC-121K Super Constellation restoration project was completed by the locally based 41st Electronic Combat Squadron. 'Project Warrior' involved the reconditioning of the aircraft for a flight to Tinker Air Force Base to complete their collection of airborne early warning and control planes. A different generation of aircraft were heading in the opposite direction as the Marine Corps began to retire some of its AV-8A and C Harrier vertical take-off aircraft in late 1985. The first arrived in August and over the next 3 years 40 more would follow.

The newly-named centre still continued its traditional mission of storage and 1986 saw the arrival of the last C-123s and O-2s in the Air Force inventory, together with over 100 T-39 Sabreliners. The last C-123, serial number 55-4547, was a UC-123K, configured for aerial spraying and it was piloted by Major-General Sloan R. Gill, chief of the Air Force Reserves. The last O-2 also arrived from the 21st Tactical Air Support Squadron. The type was built by Cessna as a replacement for the O-1 Bird Dog, and used as forward air control aircraft during the Vietnam War.

The Coast Guard began making more use of the centre and put 10 of their HC-130Bs into storage, so that the engines could be removed and fitted to new replacement HC-130s as a cost-saving measure. They were also joined by a score of Coast Guard HH-52A Sea Guard helicopters. Another 20 had arrived by the end of 1988 and they were all eventually disposed of to technical schools or target ranges.

The Air Force KC-135 Stratotanker refurbishment programme was now well underway, with 116 out of an estimated 200 civilian models purchased by the Air Force. Their engines were removed and fitted to the Air Force models, together with the airline seats, galleys, carpets and drapes. The new turbofan engines are more powerful, less noisy, less smoky and cheaper to operate. One complete cockpit assembly was donated to the Museum of Science and Technology in Tucson's sister city, Guadalajara, Mexico.

Battle Damage Repair Training is another area in which obsolete aircraft can play their part. Surplus Phantoms, Thunderchiefs and others began to depart from AMARC for repair units in Holland, England, Germany and bases throughout the United States. The aircraft are shot full of holes to simulate combat damage and are then repaired by the BDR troops, who splice new wires, make new hydraulic pipes and eventually restore the aircraft to flying shape.

Aircraft impounded by the Customs Service were also being stored at AMARC, and up to 50 small aircraft were present around this time. In addition, a Boeing 707 was parked nearby, having been seized in Galveston, Texas, loaded with mortars, machine-guns and other contraband weapons destined for Central America.

Approximately 90 Air Force Phantoms were retired between 1987 and 1988, although the total soon dropped to 68 F-4C and D models, suggesting that, for some, their stay was brief. The AMARC transportation branch was busy during 1987, with a Navy F-14 shipped out by Super Guppy to Pomona, California; Navy A-7s crated for overland shipment to Jacksonville, Florida; Navy F-8 Crusaders prepared for rail shipment to Dallas, Texas; and even a C-130 Hercules prepared for towing overland by truck. Spare parts reclamation was proceeding well and during the year 114,000 parts valued at $72 million were removed and returned to Department of Defense stocks.

It was announced that AMARC would be used to destroy ground-launched cruise missiles under the terms of the Intermediate-Range Nuclear Forces (INF) Treaty. A total of 429 Air Force Cruise missiles and more than 100 Army Pershing 2 missiles were to be destroyed. The missile warheads would be removed before the missiles arrived at AMARC and the fuel, worth $14 a gallon, would also be removed and re-used. The guidance set and jet engine can be re-used in the Navy's Tomahawk sea-launched cruise missiles. The missiles and their transporters would then be destroyed by cutting the weapons in half lengthwise, while a Soviet verification team watched the process.

AMARC also began storing production tooling for types of aircraft no longer in production, such as the A-10 ground attack aircraft and the B-1 bomber. Should the need arise to re-manufacture any component, the tooling can be located and shipped to a contractor. The tooling is coated with a product called Pro Cote 129, which is similar in appearance to clear varnish and should preserve the tooling for five to seven years.

One typical aircraft sale took place on 12 January 1988 when the Defense Reutilisation and Marketing Service offered 7 Boeing 707s and 22 Bell UH-1 helicopters for sale by tender. All were sold for scrap and the aircraft soon left for scrapyards surrounding the base. Bob Hoover's company AMCEP purchased a number of surplus Boeing 707s and Lockheed SP-2H Neptunes around this time and stored them in Bob's Airpark, just outside the perimeter of the base.

The oldest US Army Bell UH-1 Iroquois, or 'Huey' as it is universally known, was retired to AMARC on 13 September 1988. The retirement ceremony marked the start of a massive programme to retire approximately 6,000 Army aircraft over the following 20 years. Amongst the first to retire will be almost two-thirds of the UH-1 fleet, in order to make room for newer acquisitions such as the Blackhawk and Apache. With more than 3,400 Hueys in the inventory, the retirement of some 2,300 of them began towards the end of 1988. The majority will not remain in storage for long; many will be supplied to foreign armed forces or used as range targets and some will be given to local authorities.

Another Army type to begin to arrive in September 1988 was the Bell OH-58A Kiowa and 47 of the type were in storage by May 1989. Within two years they had all left again, to Corpus Christi Army Depot in Texas, for modification to OH-58D models and return to service. Just prior to the start of the Army helicopter withdrawal programme, the number of aircraft in storage had been reduced to 2,600. With the centre occupying 2,262 acres, there was plenty of room to spare.

One office at AMARC that receives little publicity is the Navy Field Service Office, a detachment of Naval Air Systems Command with half a dozen people providing administrative support for the transfer of Navy aircraft from Air Systems Command to AMARC. Towards the end of 1990 they were preparing for an influx of Grumman F-14 Tomcat fighter aircraft, following the reduction of tension in Eastern Europe and budgetary restraints leading to the reduction of the size of the squadrons. Another project was monitoring the use of vinyl bags to cover some of the Navy's Phantoms, instead of using the traditional 'Spraylat'. The bags cost $6,500 each, against more than $26,000 to process-in and maintain an F-4 for four years.

The processing of aircraft into storage has changed since the early days of the B-29s, but is no less complex a procedure. On arrival all explosives, such as ejection seat charges, are removed, together with any pilferable or particularly valuable items. The aircraft is then washed to remove industrial or marine residues and inspected for corrosion. Navy aircraft, especially those on aircraft carriers, have been exposed to corrosive salt air and require anti-corrosion treatment. The aircraft is then towed to the Preservation Section. On the process-in or flush farm, line mechanics drain the engines and hydraulic lines of oil. They also drain and reclaim the fuel from the aircraft and then pump in a lightweight oil, which is again drained, leaving a protective oil film in the lines and tanks to protect them from drying out or corroding. Engine intakes and exhausts are then covered with paper and any seams, inspection hatches, openings and rubber seals in the upper half of the aircraft are taped. The paper tape and any fragile surfaces such as canopies and radomes are then sprayed with a heavy plastic-like material called 'Spraylat', first with a black coat and then with a white coat to reflect sunlight. Wheel-wells, drainage holes and other openings under the aircraft remain open to allow the circulation of air in order to minimise condensation.

Apart from protecting the aircraft from dust, sand and the elements, the main purpose of the 'Spraylat' is to maintain the internal temperature of the aircraft at about ten to fifteen degrees hotter than the surrounding air. Without such protection the inside of an aircraft could reach 200°F, causing damage to rubber parts and functional components. Unlike the B-29 cocoon, the 'Spraylat' can be easily peeled off should the aircraft be required to fly again.

Once the preservation process is completed the aircraft is moved into the desert. Ninety days later it is inspected again to ensure the preservative is still intact, then once every 180 days until the aircraft has been stored for four years. At that time the aircraft is de-preserved and all systems are inspected to make sure there has been no damage. The method of preservation is always undergoing evaluation and AMARC has two full-time engineers in its desert laboratory undertaking research in aircraft preservation.

As AMARC looked towards the 1990s what was on the horizon? They were on the threshold of a whole new era, with defence budgets shrinking and arms agreements dictating new, lower force levels. Rough estimates of aircraft arrivals were 650 in 1990 and 400 in 1991. However, with squadrons of F-111s earmarked for retirement, 400 Phantoms looking for a new home, plus more B-52s, P-3s, A-7s and C-130s due to retire, the influx of new arrivals was expected to increase dramatically.

The Base Closure and Realignment Act passed by Congress in 1988 and the planned reorganisation of the major USAF Commands signed the death warrant for many squadrons.

Plans were underway to deactivate Military Airlift Command, Tactical Air Command and Strategic Air Command and replace them with Air Mobility Command and Air Combat Command. AMARC would report directly to Air Force Materiel Command, established on 1 July 1992 at Wright-Patterson AFB, Ohio. As a result of the down-sizing the Air Force would shrink by about 50 per cent, although some organisations would fare worse than others. Air Defense Command would find its aircraft strength reduced to about 100 aircraft in 7 Air Sovereignty Squadrons with which to defend the continental United States, where once there would have been up to 3,000.

In August 1993, 11 years after my first visit, I was back in the boneyard again. A lot had changed. Now there were 700 civilians working at AMARC, 300 more than on my first visit and 4,400 aircraft were in storage at the 2,712-acre site, 85 per cent of which were still airworthy. Approximately 100 aircraft were arriving every month, due to the reduction in size of the armed forces following the collapse of the Soviet Union. It was the biggest influx of aircraft since the end of the Vietnam War. The first thing I noticed was the B-52s; 327 of them. I was lucky to arrive when I did, for not long afterwards the slaughter of the bulk of them began, to fulfil the requirements of the START treaty. It was an eerie feeling to walk between them, camera in hand, with only the creak of ageing rudders to disturb the quiet. It felt like an elephants' graveyard; the place where old bombers come to die.

In August 1993 the AMARC inventory stood at 4,424 aircraft, almost 1,000 more that during my visit in 1982. Other items such as missiles, drones and aircraft awaiting processing brought the total inventory close to 4,800. Of these, 3,227 belonged to the Air Force, 1,454 to the Navy and Marines, 73 to the Army and 38 to the Coast Guard. There was plenty of choice for the photographer and I took 400 pictures that day, in 112 degrees of heat.

A total of 1,088 Phantoms were parked in long, straight lines; 877 from the Air Force and 211 from the Navy. Over 500 Navy and Air Force A-7s were also there, with countless variations of unit markings. Some of their old adversaries had also arrived; a dozen Polish-built MiG fighters, preserved and disassembled on pallets. They had been used by the Defense Test and Evaluation Support Agency at Kirtland AFB, New Mexico and were now earmarked for museums. Four of them have already found their way across to the Pima Air Museum, where they are displayed wearing Polish, Soviet, North Korean and North Vietnamese markings.

About a third of the aircraft in storage are expected to leave eventually, either returning to service with their original operators or other government agencies. Six former Marine OV-10 Bronco aircraft left in April 1993 for the forestry service. Designed with the forward air control role in mind, the aircraft is ideal for use in spotting fires. Other aircraft will continue their service life with foreign Air Forces, such as the Cessna O-2 Skymaster, another forward air control aircraft, which was shipped to Zimbabwe and the Ivory Coast to be used in the war against big game poachers. During my visit AT-38Bs were being prepared for flight back to Holloman AFB, New Mexico, where the 49th Fighter Wing will train pilots for the Chinese Nationalist Air Force who are purchasing a quantity. The Chilean Navy were also preparing to accept the first of half a dozen P-3 Orions and others were earmarked for Greece, Thailand, Australia and Pakistan.

I was surprised to see some F-16s in storage. I would have been even more surprised if anyone had told me that 400 of them would have been retired by the end of 1997. A dozen had arrived in 1992 straight from the factory and were being maintained in flyable hold condition. They were part of a batch purchased by

Pakistan, the sale of which had been halted by the government. Another dozen belonged to the 160th Fighter Squadron, Alabama Air National Guard, the first Guard unit to retire the type.

Newly-arrived Marine CH-53 Sea Stallion helicopters were being washed to remove any traces of corrosive salt before they joined other types in the shade of the reclamation shelter to begin the preservation process. Navy T-34 trainers, E-2 Hawkeye Airborne Early Warning aircraft and Sikorsky SH-2 helicopters were being treated during my visit and an Air Force OV-10 Bronco was being sprayed out in the open.

Because of the cutbacks in the Air Force inventory, some of the 'big guys' had started to arrive. Eight C-141 Starlifters were already in storage and two others were awaiting processing. Sixty-seven EC/KC-135s were present, together with 72 Air Force C-130s. It will be interesting to see the first C-5 Galaxy arrive; how long would it take to process one of those into storage?

Familiar faces were to be found amongst some of the rows of aircraft, such as the F-111Es carrying the 'UH' tail markings of the 20th Fighter Wing disbanded at RAF Upper Heyford in England and the 'LN' tail code of the 48th Fighter Wing F-111Es replaced at RAF Lakenheath by the F-15E. Around 180 Fairchild A-10A Thunderbolt II 'tank busters' were in storage, the majority having arrived throughout 1992. They had received their first baptism of fire not against Warsaw Pact tank columns in Central Europe, but against Saddam Hussein's Republican Guard in Kuwait and Iraq.

There were 111 civilian Boeing 707s present in varying conditions. Each cost the Air Force $900,000 and about $5 million worth of spares had been removed from each of them, so for an outlay of $99.9 million, the Air Force saved $555 million. Most of the world's 707 fleet are ending their days at AMARC and at that time almost all of TWA's airliners had moved on to the local scrapyards. Some of the airliners are being used by agencies such as the FBI and Delta Force, as well as the British and Australian Special Air Service units, to improve their anti-hijacking and aircraft disabling techniques. One story doing the rounds concerned an Ethiopian Boeing 707 that was being used for some sort of explosives exercise. Apparently it caught fire rather unexpectedly and destroyed the FBI cameras that were filming the events inside the fuselage. Another tale concerned two Royal Jordanian Cargo Boeing 707s that had arrived recently. They were found to contain civilians who had gone along for the ride, hoping to gain entry to the United States. Lacking the required paperwork to enter the country, they were rounded up and detained by local immigration officials until they could be returned whence they came. Both aircraft, together with two from Florida West Airlines and one from Anglo Cargo Airlines would later depart to Lake Charles, Louisiana, for conversion to E-8Cs.

If any one-off or interesting aircraft arrive at AMARC they are usually put on show along 'Celebrity Row' near the entrance to the storage centre. The most spectacular aircraft on display during my visit was NASA 940, a huge 'Super Guppy' based on the C-97J Stratocruiser with C-133 engines, which dwarfed everything around it. United Airlines Boeing 727 N7004U was also in the line-up pending movement to a museum and an Air Force example was parked nearby. A new type of helicopter to AMARC was parked on the row, a CH-54A Tarhe 'Flying Crane' 67-18415. This unique helicopter has a position behind the pilots, facing aft, where a third pilot would sit to control the aircraft whilst picking up a cargo load with its giant hook. A second CH-54 is now outside the entrance to the Pima Air Museum.

At the time of my visit a further 300 acres of scrubland were being cleared to handle new arrivals. One of these new arrivals was B-52G 57-6488 carrying the 'LZ' tail code of the 42nd Bomb Wing at Loring AFB, Maine. It was parked on its own, prior to joining the other 300 of the type in storage awaiting their fate. The first of them went under the guillotine on 1 October 1993. Walking amongst the B-52s I found the famous red Boeing NB-52E 56-0632 that was used by the Air Force Flight Dynamics Laboratory for Control Configured Vehicle tests before retirement in 1974. I wondered why it had been moved from 'Celebrity Row' and not shipped to a museum. The answer was not long in coming; the port side of the fuselage appeared to have been blown out by explosives and it was rendered unsafe to move. A sad waste of a suitable aircraft for preservation.

Destruction was also the fate awaiting most of the 49 Convair F-106 Delta Darts remaining in storage. With the demise of the hundreds of F-100 and F-102 remote-controlled drones at various ranges, the F-106 took their place and will eventually be followed by the F-4 Phantom.

One of the local scrapyard owners commented that the Air Force was not disposing of unwanted aircraft like it did in the old days. Times were becoming hard for the contractors who own the yards around the base perimeter. The price of aluminium had dropped from a dollar to forty cents a pound and income had to be found from other sources. Restoration of aircraft is one of them and a visit to Western International uncovered a newly-restored and painted ex-Navy C-130 and some red and white T-28s being prepared for new civilian owners.

The plight of the scrapyard owners notwithstanding, at the end of the day AMARC is an essential part of the Air Force structure. During *Desert Shield* and *Desert Storm* the centre received an influx of orders for spare parts and 1,600 items were shipped out to keep B-52s, F-111s, OV-10s, C-130s, A-7s and P-3s flying. In the fiscal year to 1992, AMARC received 996 aircraft and put 762 into storage. It withdrew more than 33,000 parts and 157 aircraft worth $680 million. Compared to AMARC's budget of $36.5 million this represented a return of more than $18 for each dollar spent. I looked out of the window of the airliner as I left Tucson airport to start my journey home, and wondered what the rest of the decade had in store for AMARC. At the rate that the US armed forces were contracting we might well find more Air Force and Navy aircraft inside AMARC than outside. Perhaps AMARC might be busier over the next few years than at any time during its distinguished career. Five years would pass before the opportunity presented itself for another visit.

It was, as usual, hot. The temperature in Tucson in October is usually in the 80s, but during the week of my visit it was around 100°F. Tuesday 13 October 1998 was going to be a good day for photographs. Armed with a new Pentax MZ-5N camera with a 28-200 zoom lens and a bag full of slide film, I duly presented myself to the guard post at the Irvington Road entrance to the base and waited for my guide to arrive. My old friend and volunteer tour guide Tech Sergeant Marc Brazil had been posted elsewhere and my AMARC friend and mentor Andy Anderson was out of town. This time my tour guide would be Terry Vanden-Huevel, a very pretty lady who runs the public affairs office at AMARC. Soon we were raising a cloud of dust with our Air Force truck as we followed the tracks towards the desert storage lots.

Five years had passed since my last visit to AMARC. A lot had happened since then. The huge fleet of B-52 bombers, 300 in number, had been reduced by two-thirds as a result of the Strategic Arms Reduction Treaty with the Soviet Union. A heavy guillotine suspended from a crane jib made short work of severing the wings and fuselage of these old bombers. The remains of these old stalwarts will lie in the open for Soviet satellites to verify their destruction, before they are then sold for scrap. As a result of the Gulf War, colourful nose art had begun to find its way back on to the cockpits of many types of aircraft, not just the bombers and fighters, but tankers and transport aircraft as well. The B-52s were no exception and it was good news to hear that almost 80 examples of *Desert Storm* nose art had been removed prior to the destruction of the aircraft. They have been sent to the Air Force Museum at Wright-Patterson Air Force Base, Ohio, where they will eventually be displayed. A list of these appear elsewhere in this book. Fortunately, a number of good examples of nose art were still to be found amidst the B-52 wrecks, one of which was the *Memphis Belle III*, successor to the famous B-17 Flying Fortress *Memphis Belle*, the first of its type to complete 25 combat missions over Nazi-occupied Europe during the Second World War.

Before we began our tour of the 2,600-acre site, at which almost 5,000 aircraft are currently stored, we paid a visit to the reclamation shelter, to observe the method of preserving artwork on aircraft arriving for storage. An A-10 Thunderbolt II was receiving its two coats of 'Spraylat' preservative, the first black and the second white. The nose art on this particular aircraft – a skull wearing a beret – had been covered with clear polythene taped down at the edges so it could still be seen and was not lost forever under a coat of preservative. Full marks should be given to the employees at AMARC for their work in preserving these examples of aviation artwork. As I started to walk down the lines of preserved aircraft later in the day, I realised just how well they had done their job.

There were three main types of artwork that I was looking for; first and foremost was traditional nose art, usually found around the nose or cockpit area of the plane. Second was graffiti, 'zaps', goodbye messages and other unusual pictures and finally came aircraft unit markings; one-off colour schemes, retirement markings, anniversary markings, test squadrons, disbanded units or anything unusual.

The F-111 storage area was a good place to start. Here I found plenty of squadron markings from units now deactivated. These included the 'Fightin' Fireball' 522nd Tactical Fighter Squadron and the 524th 'Hounds of Heaven', both belonging to the 27th Fighter Wing at Cannon AFB, New Mexico. The Wing had recently retired its EF-111A models, flown by the 429th ECS and a handful were to be found on the arrival ramp. 'The Last Deal' artwork was found covering the whole cockpit area of one F-111E that was retired by the 20th Fighter Wing in 1993, when they left the Royal Air Force base at Upper Heyford for the long flight home across the Atlantic. Some of the other F-111s wore artwork near the wing roots, such as FB-111A 68-0250 from the 380th Bomb Wing which still bore its Strategic Air Command badge and 'Silver Lady' artwork. A very good rendering of 'Angel in De Skies' was also discovered.

The KC-135 storage area also provided plenty of material. NKC-135A Stratotanker 55-3120 had been flown by the 4950th Test Wing until retirement in December 1993. It still wore the Air Force Materiel Command badge, together with 'Steam Jet One' nose art. Another NKC-135A from the same unit wore 'Aurora Explorer' nose art. One example of topical artwork was 'Stone Age Mutant Ninja Tanker' on the nose of KC-135A Stratotanker 56-3633, which was retired in August 1992 by the 305th Aerial Refueling Wing. A recent arrival, EC-135E 61-0326, was wearing 'Snoopy' artwork and the farewell message; 'Ya got all your crews home safely. What more can you ask? 1 June 98.'

The thousand-strong F-4 fleet had been reduced to just over 700, but there were quite a few good examples of artwork to be found. 'Rambo II' artwork adorns the nose of RF-4C 66-0428 which was retired by the Nebraska Air National Guard in 1993. Another RF-4C 65-0843 arrived in October 1992 wearing special markings to celebrate the 75th Anniversary of the activation of the 106th Reconnaissance Squadron, Alabama Air National Guard. Another example lamenting the end of the career of the Phantom was 64-1057 wearing 'Phantoms Phorever' artwork to mark the retirement of the type in 1994. Another interesting Phantom found near the arrival ramp was repainted specially for the visit of Major-General Steve Ritchie, the only ace from the Vietnam War still serving in the Air Force. The Phantom wore five stars to commemorate his five MiG-kills and underneath the General wrote 'Can it possibly be 25 years? Steve Ritchie 3 Oct 1997.' With the Phantom providing the next generation of target drones, one hopes that steps will be taken to preserve some of the more interesting artwork before it is too late.

One surprise amongst the 50 C-141 Starlifters now in storage was NC-141A 61-2776, which was operated by the Air Force Flight Test Centre at Edwards Air Force Base. It was found to be wearing expertly drawn 'Desert Rat' artwork and farewell signatures from pilots and crew.

The record for the oldest artwork or markings found at AMARC must go to Lockheed SP-2H Neptune 147963 which still wears the Patron 69 badge of Navy Patrol Squadron VP-69, from which it was retired in 1975. Another SP-2H, 148340, which was retired in 1976 still wears a good example of the badge of Navy Patrol Squadron VP-94, along with the irreverent inscription 'Nellie Blowjob' on the lower fuselage. The only Navy Douglas C-118B Liftmaster currently in storage has also been around a while, having been retired in 1982. It still wears the badge of Fleet Logistic Support Squadron VR-51.

The 380 F-16 Fighting Falcons now in storage include examples from every Air National Guard unit that has ever operated the type, each with their own state markings. They have now been joined by 18 Navy TF/F-16N models that were operated by Navy Fighter Squadrons VF-43 and VF-45 and the Naval Fighter Weapons School. Red and white painted F-16s were also to be found, from Edwards Air Force Base where they flew with the 412th Test Wing. Although many F-16s have arrived for storage since 1992, a small number have departed in the opposite direction. On 7 January 1996 an agreement was reached between the US Secretary of State William Perry and the late King Hussein of Jordan on the transfer of 16 F-16A/Bs to that country following President Clinton's declaration that Jordan had been elected as a major non-NATO ally of the United States. Known as the Peace Falcon Program, the deal saw the 16 former Air National Guard aircraft shipped from AMARC to the Ogden Air Logistics Center at Hill AFB, Utah, for overhaul and improvement prior to delivery. Pilot training was scheduled to take place with the Arizona Air National Guard at nearby Tucson International Airport.

Almost 200 Bell UH-1 Hueys are in storage, two thirds belonging to the Army, the rest to the Navy and Air Force. Sadly the Army models were generally lacking in artwork, unlike the days of the Vietnam War when practically all Army helicopters wore some kind of artwork. UH-1H 63-8748 was still wearing a shield and the inscription *Qui Transtulit Sustinet* when it was retired by the Connecticut National Guard in 1995. Does anyone know the translation? Navy HH-1N 158233 still wore a good example of the US Naval Air Station Bermuda badge, despite the full preservation treatment that it received on arrival in May 1995. One interesting Cobra in storage is AH-1J 3-4412 of the Imperial Iranian Army, complete with desert camouflage scheme. It has been in storage since June 1980, presumably as a result of some kind of arms embargo.

Over 130 Navy P-3 Orions are in storage including a couple from Navy Oceanographic Development Squadron VXN-8, one of which is UP-3A 150527 decorated with 'Tasmanian Devil' artwork, albeit slightly faded after nine years in the desert sun. Its sister ship, 152176, wears 'Arctic Fox' artwork. It was the only military squadron dedicated to airborne geophysical surveying.

The number of F-106 Delta Darts in storage have dwindled to about a score, but they include a handful that had previously departed for conversion to QF-106 drones and have recently returned for storage. Examples include 59-0043 which wears the badges of all of the various units which have flown the type, including the 82nd Tactical Aerial Target Squadron at Tyndall AFB, Florida. As is usual with converted drones, they also have their tails and wingtips painted red.

The Navy has now retired the last of its A-6 Intruders and there were many examples of rare markings or artwork to be found. A-6E 155698 wears the markings of VX-5, the Weapon Test Squadron at China Lake, California. Access to this base has always been difficult and photos of the based aircraft hard to come by. Two of the A-6Es are from Navy Attack Squadron VA-75 who flew the first Intruders in combat during the Vietnam War. One of them wears 'Last of the Intruders' artwork from its recent tour of duty on USS *Enterprise*, the other is painted in original VA-75 markings from its 1965 tour on the USS *Independence*. If you look hard enough you might find one or two A-6s with full-colour tail markings, unusual in these days of subdued markings. One, A-6E 159579, was specially painted for the use of the Commander Air Group of CVW-14.

Sixty of the Navy's FA-18 Hornets are now in storage, including a couple of very colourful examples from the Naval Fighter Weapons School that were amongst the first to arrive in April 1995. Known as 'Top Gun' the NFWS trains fighter crews in all aspects of fighter and adversary operation at Miramar Naval Air Station, California.

The Navy loaned two of their E-2C Hawkeye airborne early warning aircraft to the Coast Guard for drug-smuggler detection duties, one of which was put into storage in 1992. It wears the 'Just Say No' catch-phrase of the anti-drug campaign sponsored by former First Lady Nancy Reagan.

Around 80 C-130 Hercules transport aircraft are in storage. One superb example is a ski-equipped LC-130R which was retired in July 1997 by Navy Antarctic Development Squadron VXE-6. This rarely seen aircraft is painted in high-visibility markings to aid searchers if it was unfortunate enough to go down on the ice. Another unusual model was AC-130A gunship 54-1628 wearing 'The Exterminator' artwork and the badge of the 919th Special Operations Wing, Air Force Reserve. We also came across another version of the *Memphis Belle* artwork, this time on the port side of C-130A 57-0463 which served with the 164th Tactical Airlift Group, Tennessee Air National Guard until retirement in 1992.

Some newer types had arrived for storage wearing nose art. Swearingen C-26B Metro 23 91-0510 had been used as a mission support aircraft by the 114th Fighter Wing, South Dakota Air National Guard, and arrived for storage in September 1997. It still wears 'Four Presidents' artwork in black and white. Another new guy was Boeing T-43A 73-1155 wearing the 'RA' tail code denoting Randolph Air Force Base, Texas, and 'The Spirit of San Antonio' artwork on the nose.

The most recent examples of artwork to arrive must be on the OA-10A Thunderbolt IIs of the 19th Fighter Squadron, 51st Fighter Wing, which have just started arriving from South Korea. They wear the 'OS' tail code to denote Osan Air Force Base and a black horse painted just behind the cockpit.

As the accompanying photographs will testify, the visit was very successful. There can be no doubt that the fate of the aviation artwork passing through AMARC is in safe hands. Perhaps the saving of the B-52 artwork is only the beginning? Time will tell. Maybe efforts can be made to remove artwork as a matter of course before aircraft are sold for scrap.

Many of the aircraft stored at AMARC eventually pass through one of the local scrapyards and at the time of the author's visit in October 1998 quite a lot of movements had been taking place. Dross Metals Inc still contains a number of old inmates including a score of C-117s and 35 A-4C/L Skyhawks which have been there for over a decade, having been sold originally to the Royal Malaysian Air Force. Newer types to be seen are ten ex-Navy C-130s, which once served with VQ-4, but have now been allocated civilian registrations. Some of the residents are rather rare and include a C-97, C-119, two HU-16s and a C-133 Cargomaster.

Western International are usually very busy and recent work has included the conversion of three C-131Fs to mosquito sprayers; the processing of former Navy SH-3H Sea Kings for the civil market, including a pair for the Los Angeles County Sheriffs Department to replace its elderly Sikorsky S-58Ts at Long Beach Municipal Airport; ex-Marine OV-10 Broncos being converted as fire spotters for the California Department of Forestry and the shipment of CT-39 Sabreliners to technical schools and colleges.

So what does the future hold for AMARC? The US Navy plan to standardise their helicopter fleet with the purchase of up to 250 Sikorsky CH-60S Sea Hawk helicopters. These will replace types such as the HH-1N, UH/VH-3H and the CH/HH/UH-46D Sea Knight, so presumably all of these will eventually find their way to AMARC. Meanwhile the Navy's existing fleet of Sea Hawks, consisting of SH-60B, SH-60F and HH-60H models, will be remanufactured to a common SH-60R specification.

Large numbers of surplus US Army helicopters are currently reaching the civilian market, although not all of them are going through AMARC. One company involved is A and S Helicopters Inc of St Louis Downtown-Park Airport, Illinois, which is currently overhauling OH-6 and OH-58 helicopters for resale to Federal and State agencies. The disposal of older types of Army helicopter is expected to continue for some years yet.

As far as the Air Force is concerned, they have found a customer for the 28 F-16A/Bs that were originally destined for Pakistan in the early 1990s. New Zealand has agreed to lease all the aircraft to replace their ageing A-4 Skyhawks. The first aircraft is not expected to be delivered for at least 2 years and 4 will be kept at AMARC as attrition replacements and 2 others will be cannibalised for spare parts. All the aircraft were sent direct to AMARC from the production line, with the first arriving on 10 April 1992, following an embargo on the sale.

AMARC expects its inventory to remain at approximately 5,000 aircraft for the foreseeable future. They also expect a continued emphasis on Foreign Military Sale aircraft withdrawal over the next several years. Reclamation will continue to see emphasis on programmed and priority reclamation due to limited funding and availability of parts from normal supply sources. In the fiscal year 1997 AMARC reclaimed 26,992 aircraft parts and delivered them to their customers in an average time of 7.2 days. They are continually striving to shorten delivery times and to provide eventually a 'parts on demand' service. Yes, AMARC is an impressive place run by friendly people and situated in one of the nicest states in the Union. If you don't believe me, go and see for yourself. Tell them I sent you.

Below: The author (centre) with sons Mark (left) and Peter (right) standing by the remains of B-52G Stratofortress 'Lucky 13' 58-0236, retired by 2nd Wing, Air Combat Command, in October 1992. The wing was based at Barksdale AFB in California.

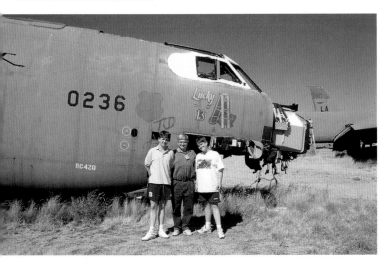

Above: A caped figure and a whale are featured on the tail of this EA-3B Skywarrior 146448, which used to fly with Fleet Air Reconnaissance Squadron VQ-2 until its retirement in September 1991. The last operational 'Whale' squadron in the Navy, the 'Batmen' of VQ-2 subsequently equipped with the EP-3E electronic warfare aircraft.

Below: Navy Douglas UA-3B Skywarrior 144834/2A125 still wears its red star markings from its time with Tactical Electronic Warfare Squadron VAQ-34. The squadron carries out an aggressor role to train land-based and shipboard radar operators in tracking hostile aircraft. It arrived for storage in September 1990.

A row of colourful Navy TA-4J Skyhawk trainers from Training Wing TW-2 which arrived in the summer of 1994. Nearest to the camera is 155076/3A829 'B-106'. A row of Air Force T-38 trainers can be seen in the background.

U.S.N.T.P.S.

Left and below: TA-4J Skyhawk 153524/3A809 '08' from the Navy Test Pilots School heads this row of Skyhawks. It arrived in August 1994 and appears to be devoid of 'Spraylat' and in good condition after five years in storage.

Right and below: The badge of the Naval Air Test Center, is seen on OA-4M Skyhawk 154306/3A600 'SD-02', which arrived in May 1991 from Patuxent River, Maryland.

Grumman A-6E Intruder 155698/5A223 was flown by the Weapons Test Squadron VX-5 at China Lake Naval Air Warfare Center Weapons Division in California (formerly the Naval Weapons Test Center) until its retirement in September 1996. Note the varied tail markings on the A-6s in the background.

Above: Special care was taken to preserve the 'Boxer' nose art on this A-6E Intruder. It is 162179 'AA-501' from Navy Attack Squadron VA-75 and arrived in March 1997.

Opposite above: A-6E Intruder 155662 'NF-500' of Navy Attack Squadron VA-115 arrived in July 1996 wearing these colourful markings. 'The Eagles' of VA-115 joined the aircraft carrier USS *Independence* in 1991 when it became home-ported with Carrier Air Wing CVW-5 at Yokosuka, Japan.

Opposite below: 'Last of the Intruders' tail markings are present on A-6E 161662 whose last cruise was with Navy Attack Squadron VA-75 on USS *Enterprise*. The next A-6E in line, 157027, also wears VA-75 markings to commemorate its first tour on the USS *Independence* in 1965. Both arrived at AMARC in March 1997. VA-75 'The Sunday Punchers' was the first Fleet squadron to operate the Intruder during the Vietnam War.

Left: A 'Road Runner' clutching two bombs is featured in the squadron markings of this New Mexico Air National Guard A-7D, 75-388/AE198, which arrived in August 1992 after serving with the 188th Fighter Squadron, 150th Fighter Group.

Opposite above: 'Black Cat' nose art is present on EA-6B Prowler 158542/5A132 which arrived for storage from Grumman in September 1994. Note the field of P-3 Orions in the distance.

Opposite below: Nine years in the sun has faded the paintwork on TA-7C 154377 revealing its old 'NJ' tail markings. It later served as '06' with VAQ-34, an aggressor unit based at Naval Air Station Point Mugu, California.

Below: Now with its cockpit assembly removed, this A-10A Thunderbolt II 75-297 served with the 357th Fighter Squadron, 355th Fighter Wing, at Davis-Monthan Air Force Base and was retired in May 1992.

Left and below: This FA-18A Hornet was the first of its type to arrive for storage in June 1994. Wearing the inventory code 1A001, it last served with Navy Fighter Attack Squadron VFA-303 'The Golden Hawks' at Naval Air Station Leemore, California. Their squadron emblem depicts a hawk against a hostile sky.

Opposite above: The nose art on this OA-10A Thunderbolt II has been saved from oblivion by this AMARC employee who has begun to spray the second, white coat of 'Spraylat' preservative on the aircraft. AC137 is 77-0266 which was retired by the 706th Fighter Squadron (which wears the 'NO' tail code) in October 1992. It has been inspected and was being re-preserved in October 1998.

Opposite below: Arriving on the day of the author's visit in October 1998, this OA-10A Thunderbolt II 79-211 served with the 19th Fighter Squadron, 51st Fighter Wing, at Osan Air Base, Republic of Korea. Note the black horse just behind the cockpit.

Above: 'Memphis Belle III' nose art is featured on B-52G Stratofortress 59-2594, which was retired by the 2nd Wing in October 1992. The unit motto is *Libertatem Defendimus* – Liberty We Defend'. B-52Gs were responsible for dropping more than one third of all ordnance unloaded by USAF aircraft on Iraq during the 1991 Gulf War.

Opposite above: Photographed on the arrival ramp in April 1995, FA-18A Hornet 161716 '70' bears the NFWS (Navy Fighter Weapons School) name and badge on its fin. Known as 'Top Gun' the NFWS trains fighter crews in all aspects of fighter and adversary operation at Miramar Naval Air Station, California.

Opposite below: Its markings beginning to fade after six years in storage in the desert sun, B-52G Stratofortress 57-6471 wears 'Tantalizing Takeoff' artwork and displays a view normally only seen by maintenance crews.

Above: Saved from destruction and now preserved at the nearby Pima Air Museum, NB-52A Stratofortress 52-0003 has 'The High and Mighty One' fuselage markings which record launches of the X-15 experimental aircraft. The cradle in which it was carried can be seen under the wing.

Opposite above: Lost forever, Boeing NB-52E Stratofortress 56-0632 arrived for storage in June 1974 after use by Boeing and the Air Force Flight Dynamics Laboratory for Control Configured Vehicle tests. Instead of preserving the nose art, preferably with the cockpit section attached, the Air Force allowed the aircraft to be used for explosive tests at AMARC and it was later scapped.

Opposite below: 'Triple Deuce' artwork is featured on this 2nd Bomb Wing B-52G, 58-0222. Its last flight to AMARC took place on 12 August 1992 and it was recently eliminated as a part of the START arms reduction treaty after a total of 16,560 flight hours. The nose art was cut out and sent to the Air Force Museum where it will eventually be displayed along with others which suffered a similar fate.

Above: Grumman TC-4C Acadame 155729 was the first of the type to arrive for storage in April 1994 after service with Navy Attack Squadron VA-42. The squadron used four of the type as radar systems trainers in support of A-6 Intruder communities of both Navy and Marine Corps.

Opposite above: The massive wings of this WB-57F Canberra are shown to advantage in this photograph of NASA 925 'Earth Survey 3', now on display at the Pima Air Museum. Its previous USAF serial number is 63-13501 and it was retired to AMARC in September 1982.

Opposite below: Grumman C-1A Trader 146038 served on the USS *Lexington* until its retirement in May 1986. It is earmarked for the National Museum of Naval Aviation, Pensacola, Florida.

Above: Parked in Flyable Hold condition with minimum protection from the sun, this Short Brothers C-23A Sherpa, 84-0458, arrived from the 412th Test Wing with two others in December 1997. The tail code 'ED' is applied to aircraft based at the Air Force Flight Test Center, Edwards AFB, California.

Opposite above and below: 'Four Presidents' artwork is present on this Swearingen C-26B Metro 23, serial number 91-0510. Used as a mission support aircraft by the 114th Fighter Wing, South Dakota Air National Guard, it is one of four currently in storage in Flyable Hold. Note the lack of 'Spraylat' preservative.

The latest addition to the Air Force transport fleet, these two McDonnell Douglas C-27As, 91-0107 and 90-0173, arrived in September 1997. Both belong to the 24th Wing whose 'HW' tail code denotes its base – Howard AFB, Panama. They are kept in Flyable Hold condition with minimum preservation.

This photograph illustrates the effect on the centre of gravity of an aircraft when its engines are removed. Douglas C-118B Liftmaster 131568 was retired by Navy Fleet Logistic Support Squadron VR-51 in September 1982. The squadron badge can be seen to the right of the '568'. Note the Phantom with its cockpit removed in the background.

Right and below: Another version of the 'Memphis Belle' artwork. This time it is featured on the port side of C-130A Hercules 57-0463 which served with the 164th Tactical Airlift Group, Tennessee Air National Guard, until its retirement in January 1992.

Following the end of US Navy participation in Operation *Deep Freeze*, this ski-equipped LC-130R Hercules was retired by Navy Antarctic Development Squadron VXE-6 to AMARC in July 1997 and is currently parked on Celebrity Row.

Below: Boeing OC-135B Stratotanker 61-2674 was retired by the Offutt AFB, Nebraska-based 55th Wing in August 1997. The aircraft flown by the wing are used in the airborne command and control and strategic reconnaissance roles.

Opposite above and below: Slightly faded after three years in storage, this 'Spectre' artwork is still visible on 'The Exterminator' AC-130A Hercules gunship 54-1628. Also visible is the badge of its last operator, the 919th Special Operations Wing, Air Force Reserve.

Above and opposite: 'Steam Jet One' nose art on NKC-135A Stratotanker 55-3120, together with Air Force Materiel Command badge. Previously flown by the 4950th Test Wing at Wright Patterson AFB, Ohio, it was retired in December 1993.

Above and right: A recent arrival from Air Force Materiel Command, Boeing EC-135E 61-0326 is adorned with 'Snoopy' artwork and the farewell message, 'Ya got all your crews home safely. What more can you ask? 1 June 98.'

Below: 'Aurora Explorer' artwork is present on the port side of NKC-135A Stratotanker CA053/55-3131, which was retired by the 4950th Test Wing in October 1992.

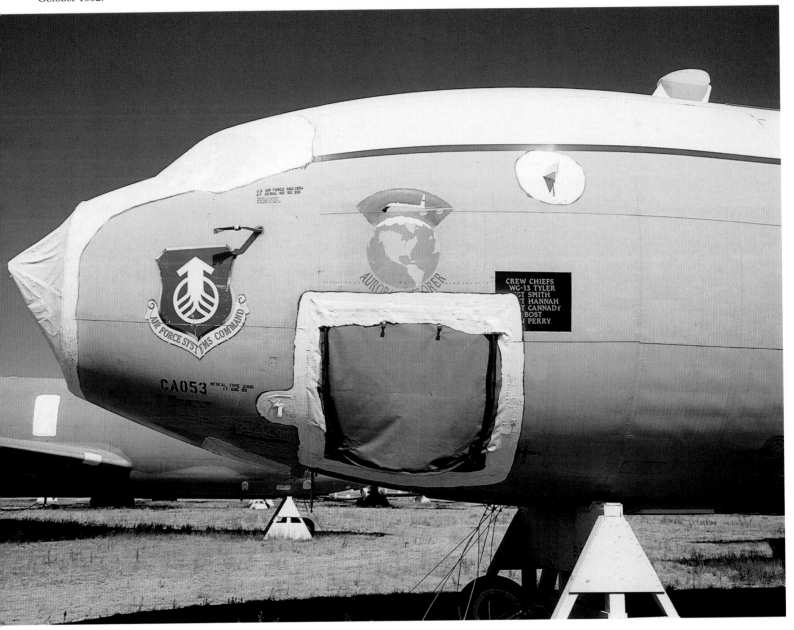

Above: The badge of the 4950th Test Wing on the starboard side of NKC-135A 55-3131.

Opposite above and below: Boeing KC-135A Stratotanker 62-3532 wears 'DY' on the tail, denoting Dyess AFB, Texas. The *E Sempre L'ora* (It is always the hour) shield of the 96th Wing is on its nose, together with Texas turtle nose art. The aircraft served with the 917th Aerial Refueling Squadron until its retirement in August 1993.

Below: 'Pirate' nose art is present on KC-135A Stratotanker 58-0097, retired by the 19th Aerial Refueling Wing in September 1992.

Above: Retired in May 1993, Boeing KC-135A Stratotanker 56-3625 wears 'Boss Hog' nose art and the 96th Wing's shield, featuring a falcon's head with a bomb in its beak and the motto *'E Sempre L'ora* – It is always the hour'.

Opposite above: 'Freedom's Best' nose art is present on KC-135A Stratotanker 56-3634, retired in August 1992 by the 305th Aerial Refueling Wing. EC-135G 63-7994 can be seen in the background.

Opposite below: 'Big Bad Boom' nose art is featured on KC-135A Stratotanker 56-3637, flown by the 305th Aerial Refueling Wing until its retirement in August 1992. Note the 'Aladdin's lamp' zaps above the wooden fuselage-support representing refuelling missions during the Gulf War.

Above: Boeing KC-135A 62-3501 from the 97th Air Mobility Wing wears a
'Young Tiger S.E. Asia 1964–1973' badge commemorating its support of
Strategic Air Command combat operations in Southeast Asia during which
it furnished aircraft and crews to other organisations. The aircraft arrived
at AMARC in July 1993.

Opposite above: Recent arrival NC-141A Starlifter 61-2776/CR0055 wears
expertly drawn 'Desert Rat' artwork and farewell signatures from pilots
and crew. It was recently operated by the Air Force Flight Test Center,
Edwards Air Force Base, California.

Opposite below: A new arrival photographed at the fuel flush farm in
October 1998, C-141B Starlifter 65-0223/CR0058 wears the Air Education
and Training Command badge on its starboard side and the red and yellow
fin stripe of the 97th Air Mobility Wing, based at Altus AFB, Oklahoma.

Some fifty C-141 Starlifters are currently in storage, including C-141B 67-0023 from the 356th Airlift Squadron, Air Force Reserve, based at Wright Patterson AFB, Ohio. Fatigue became a problem for the C-141s and the long-awaited C-17 Globemaster III replacement programme is underway.

'Just Say NO' was the catch-phrase of the anti-drugs campaign sponsored by former First Lady Nancy Reagan. This Grumman E-2C Hawkeye 160415/2E023 was one of a pair on loan from the Navy for drug-smuggling detection duties. It was retired in November 1992.

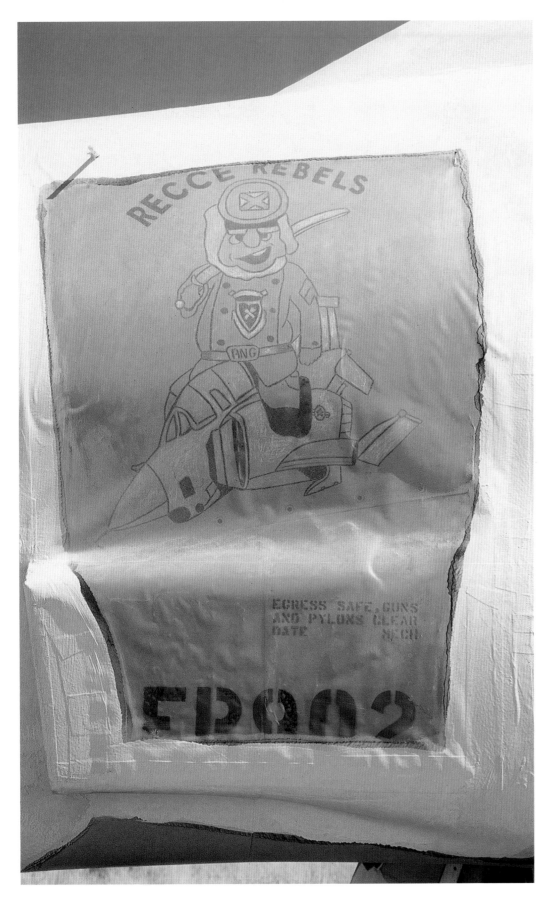

This spread: Probably the most 'decorated' Phantom in AMARC, RF-4C 65-0843/FP902 arrived in October 1992. Preserved on the nose is 'Recce Rebels' artwork; on the tail 'Birmingham' denotes the Alabama base for the 106th Reconnaissance Squadron, 117th Reconnaissance Wing, Air National Guard. The unit was celebrating the 75th anniversary of its activation in August 1917.

Above: A view of the departure ramp, photographed in October 1998, showing F-4 Phantoms being prepared for departure and conversion to target drones. Note the two dice on the top of the fin of the nearest aircraft, F-4E 69-0290, wearing the 'PN' code of the 3rd Tactical Fighter Wing which retired the aircraft in January 1991. The next aircraft in line is F-4G 69-0292 wearing 'WW', denoting its Wild Weasel role, and 562FS on the fin. It was retired by the 562nd Fighter Squadron, 35th Fighter Wing, in July 1992. Note the squadron badge visible just above the mobile ground power unit.

Opposite above and below: 'Phantoms Phorever' laments the 'Pharewell' of the Phantoms in 1994. 64-1057 'BH' was retired by the 106th Reconnaissance Squadron, Alabama Air National Guard, in May 1994. The unit converted from the RF-84F to the Phantom in 1971.

Above and opposite: This F-4 was repainted specially for the visit of Major-General Steve Ritchie, the only ace from the Vietnam War still in the Air Force. He wrote under the five MiG-kills 'Can it possibly be 25 years? Steve Ritchie 3 Oct 1997.'

35TH TAC TRNG SQ

4443 TTS

AIR WARRIOR

21 TFS

20 TFTS

M.P. TYPE
RIL. 30. 1990

M.P. TYPE 1000
MAR. 22 1995

M.P. TYPE 1000

M.P. TYPE 1000
28 OCT 92

M.P. TYPE 1000
OCT 07 1993

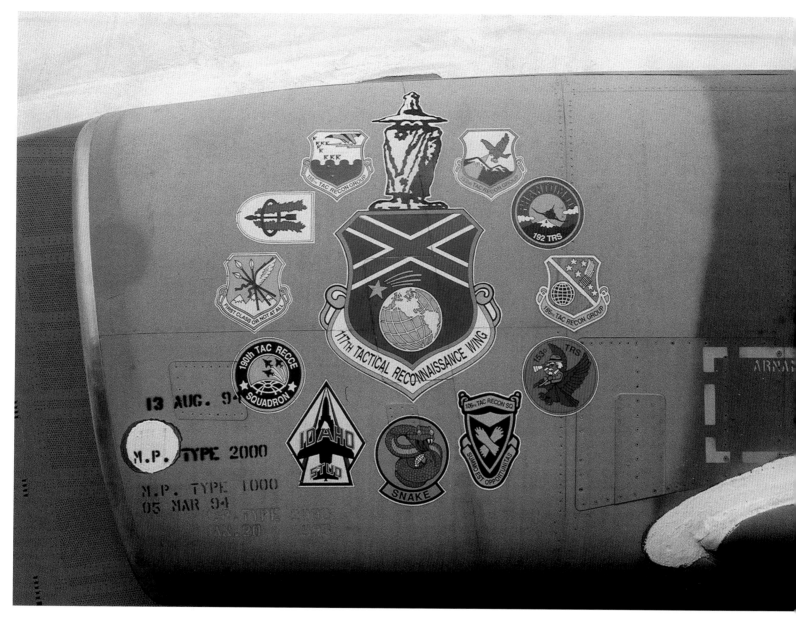

Above: Retired in August 1993, RF-4C Phantom 65-0854 from the Birmingham, Alabama-based 117th Tactical Reconnaissance Wing which celebrated its twentieth year of operating the Phantom in 1991. The wing badge is surrounded by patches from other units which operated the type.

Opposite above: F-4E Phantom 66-0357/FP392 wears the faded tail markings 'GA' 35TTW and the badges of the wing's units on the port air intake. It was previously based at George Air Force Base in California and arrived at AMARC in November 1989.

Opposite below: Badges of the 20th TFTS, 21st TFS, 4443rd TTS and 35th TTS are on F-4E 66-0357, previously operated by the 35th Tactical Training Wing.

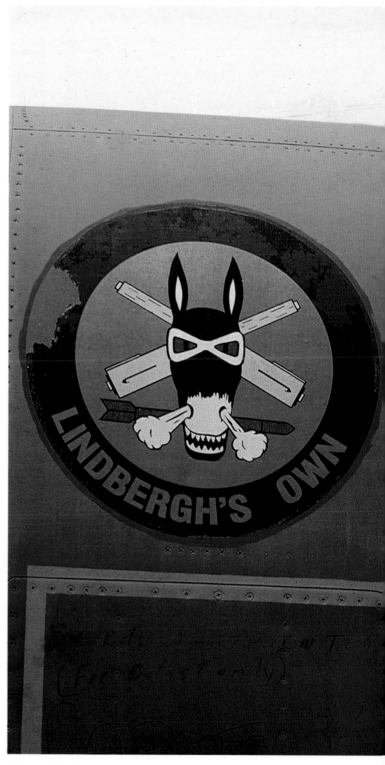

RF-4C Phantom 66-0428/FP944 with its 'Rambo II' nose art was retired by the 173rd Reconnaissance Squadron, Nebraska Air National Guard in September 1993. The squadron belonged to the 155th Reconnaissance Group based at Lincoln Airport, Nebraska.

The 'Lindbergh's Own' badge is featured on F-4E Phantom 67-370 'SL' from the 110th Tactical Fighter Squadron, Missouri Air National Guard, which arrived in August 1991. The 'snorting mule' insignia was approved on 7 July 1949 when the unit was equipped with F-51D Mustangs.

'Way to go Alabama!' Diamond Jubilee artwork on the nose of this RF-4C has been thoughtfully preserved by the guys in the 'Spraylat' shelter. The Alabama Air National Guard was celebrating 25 years of Phantom operations.

Above: 'Recce Rebels' artwork is featured on this RF-4C Phantom from the 106th Reconnaissance Squadron, Alabama Air National Guard, based at Birmingham International Airport. The unit was celebrating the 75th anniversary of its formation.

Opposite above and below: The 'Top Hatters' of Navy Fighter Squadron VF-14 flew their F-14A Tomcats from the USS *John F Kennedy* during Operation *Desert Storm*. 159863 'AJ-216' was the 100th of the type to be stored in April 1997. It is now parked on Celebrity Row.

Above: A line of Navy F-14A Tomcats, the nearest wearing the markings of Navy Fighter Squadron VF-101, the 'Grim Reapers'. The next three belong to VF-32, the 'Swordsmen', based with VF-101 at Oceana Naval Air Station, Virginia.

Opposite above and below: F-15A Eagle 76-0030/FH075 was retired in April 1994 by the 110th Fighter Squadron, Missouri Air National Guard. The squadron belonged to the 131st Fighter Wing based at Lambert Field, St Louis, across the runway from the McDonnell Douglas plant which produced the Eagle.

This F-15A Eagle belonged to the commanding officer of the 131st Fighter Wing and arrived for storage in December 1994. The tail code 'SL' denotes its base at St Louis, Missouri.

A row of F-16 Fighting Falcon tails. F-16A 81-0675/FG360 from the 179th Fighter Squadron is nearest and wears Duluth markings; its base was at Duluth International Airport, Minnesota. The tail markings signify the North Star and Little Dipper to reflect its north-facing defence role. Next in line is F-16B 78-0082/FG381 from 162nd Fighter Wing, Arizona Air National Guard.

Right and below: The tail markings on 119th Fighter Squadron, New Jersey Air National Guard F-16A Fighting Falcon 81-0715 show an 'Atlantic City' badge. A Florida ANG F-16 is next in line.

Navy F-16N Fighting Falcon 163571, wearing the inventory code FG430, arrived in March 1998. Two other examples are parked nearby, with 163574 nearest. Both were retired from Navy Fighter Squadron VF-43 in June 1994. Based at Oceana Naval Air Station, Virginia, the squadron is an aggressor outfit providing dissimilar air combat training.

Above: Photographed on the arrival ramp in July 1995, this two-seater F-16B has just arrived from Edwards Air Force Base, California, where it flew with the 412th Test Wing.

Opposite above: F-106A Delta Dart 59-0043 was retired by the New Jersey Air National Guard in 1988 and allocated the AMARC inventory number FN194. It departed in December 1992 for conversion to a QF-106A target drone. It has recently returned for storage and now wears the inventory code FN207.

Opposite below: This close-up of F-106A Delta Dart 59-0043 shows all of the various units which have flown the type, including the 82nd Tactical Aerial Targets Squadron at Tyndall AFB, Florida. AD227 is its post-conversion to QF-106A serial number.

Below: The 'Desert Sand' test paintwork on F-111D 68-0112/FV114 from the 523rd Fighter Squadron, 27th Fighter Wing, has faded to a pink colour since its arrival for storage in August 1992.

Opposite above and below: The 'Last Deal' nose art on this F-111E commemorates the deactivating, in 1993, of the 77th Fighter Squadron of the Royal Air Force. The Squadron, based at Upper Heyford, England, was part of the 20th Fighter Wing which had operated F-111Es since 1970.

Above: F-111D 68-0101, together with the other camouflaged models in the background, was retired by the 27th Fighter Wing at Cannon Air Force Base, New Mexico, in 1991/2. The aircraft wears the badge of the 522nd Fighter Squadron.

Opposite above: BF013 is FB-111A 68-0250 from the 380th Bomb Wing, and was retired in July 1991. The Strategic Air Command badge and 'Silver Lady' artwork have withstood eight years in the desert sun.

Opposite below: The 'Farewell' artwork on the nose of F-111F 74-0187 commemorates its retirement from the 27th Fighter Wing at Cannon Air Force Base, New Mexico, in September 1996. Note the 524th Squadron badge near the AMARC inventory code FV0301.

Above: Now resident at the Pima Air Museum, Tucson, F-111E 68-0033 still wears the bomb mission artwork representing its participation in Operation *Desert Storm*.

Opposite above: 'Moonlight Maid' artwork on one of the many F-111s in storage during the author's visit in October 1998.

Opposite below: A very skilful rendering of 'Angel in de Skies' was found on an F-111 at AMARC in October 1998.

Above: A long-term resident of AMARC, Bell AH-1J Cobra 7H090 carries the Imperial Iranian Army serial number 3-4412 on its tail boom. It arrived for storage in June 1980.

Opposite above and below: The California Department of Forestry shield is visible on the starboard door of this Bell UH-1F Huey. A former Air Force machine, its serial number 65-7917 has been painted over. It arrived at AMARC in September 1996.

Opposite above and below: This Army UH-1H Huey, 63-8748, was retired by the Connecticut Army National Guard in October 1995. The shield on the door bears the Latin inscription '*Qui Transtulit Sustinet*'. Note the cable cutting device above the windshield.

Left and below: A United States Naval Air Station Bermuda badge is on Bell HH-1N Huey 158233, which was given the full preservation treatment on its arrival in May 1995.

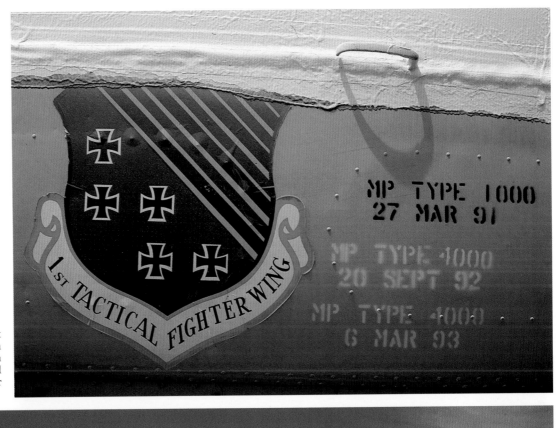

Right and below: The badge of the 1st Tactical Fighter Wing is featured on UH-1P Huey 63-13149/HF176, which arrived in December 1987. Established in 1947, the wing motto is 'Conquer or die'.

Retired in December 1994, SH-3H Sea King 148999 was last flown by Helicopter Anti-submarine Squadron HS-4 on the USS *Iwo Jima*. The markings on the nose may signify space capsule recoveries. The unit re-equipped with the Sikorsky SH-60F Seahawk.

Above: NASA 735 is Sikorsky SH-3G Sea King 149723, which arrived in July 1993. Note the nose-mounted radar.

Opposite above and below: Sikorsky SH-3G Sea King 148970 served with Navy Helicopter Combat Support Squadron HC-2 Detachment 2 until its retirement in November 1993. Although the squadron was based at Naval Air Station Norfolk, Virginia, it maintained a pair of SH-3Gs, known as 'Desert Duck Airlines' on permanent detachment in Bahrain. Would any reader care to translate the Arabic script on the port sponson?

Opposite above: Sikorsky HH-52A Sea Guard 1450 'Houston' was retired by the Coast Guard to AMARC in February 1989. It spent only six weeks there before moving across the road to the Pima Air Museum where it remains today.

Opposite below: This CH-53E Super Stallion, 161542, was flown by Helicopter Combat Support Squadron HC-4, the 'Black Stallions', until its retirement in September 1995. The squadron was based at Sigonella Naval Air Station, Italy, to provide support for Mediterranean Fleet activities, including missions to provide relief for Kurdish refugees in Western Iraq.

Left: Still wearing its sand camouflage paint scheme, Marines CH-53D Sea Stallion 156655 carried the 'YH-14' code of Marine Helicopter Squadron, Heavy HMH-463, when it was retired in November 1993. Elements of the 'Heavy Haulers' squadron deployed to King Abdul Aziz naval air base, Saudi Arabia, during Operation *Desert Storm*.

Below: The huge sponsons on this H-53 contain extra fuel and identify it as MH-53E Sea Dragon 162511 from Helicopter Mine Countermeasures Squadron HM-15 (the 'Blackhawks'), which arrived for storage in June 1995. The aircraft is capable of carrying out a four-hour mine-sweeping mission.

Above and left: This Lockheed SP-2H Neptune wears the 'Patron 69' badge of Navy Patrol Squadron VP-69 and has been in storage since 1975. It is currently held for the Smithsonian Institute with the new inventory code LF0001.

Opposite above and below: 'World Traveler' Lockheed UP-3A Orion 150527 was retired by Navy Oceanographic Development Squadron VXN-8 in April 1990. It was the only military squadron dedicated to airborne geophysical surveying. Note the line of Phantoms in protective bags in the background. The 'Tasmanian Devil' artwork on the front of the aircraft is suffering from nine years of exposure to the desert sun.

Opposite above: Three separate variations of the Navy Antisubmarine Warfare Squadron VS-38 'Red Griffin' can be seen on these S-3A Vikings. Two of the aircraft have their tails folded in the shipboard storage mode.

Opposite below: A line of North American T-2C Buckeye trainers, with 159708/2T197 nearest, wearing the 'F-817' code of Carrier Training Wing CTW-6. The aircraft was retired in June 1992. The type first entered Navy service in 1959.

Left: The badge of the 84th Fighter Interceptor Training Squadron – a black cat and two streaks of lightning – is worn by Lockheed T-33A Shooting Star 57-0759 which arrived in February 1987.

Below: Lockheed T-33A Shooting Star 58-2099/TC1320 arrived in February 1987, wearing the markings of the 5th Fighter Interceptor Squadron. The unit also flew the F-106 out of Minot Air Force Base, North Dakota.

Above: TE106 is T-37B Tweety Bird 59-0294, which was retired by the 366th Wing in September 1995. The unit badge carries the motto '*Audentes Fortuna Juvat* – Fortune favours the bold'.

Left and below: T-38A Talon 66-4383/TF318 arrived for storage in February 1996. The words 'Barksdale' and 'LA' on the tail denote its last home as Barksdale Air Force Base, Louisiana, the headquarters of the 8th Air Force.

Right and below: An unusual arrival in October 1994 was T-38A Talon 62-3652/TF279 'MO', wearing the red and black shield of the 366th Wing on its nose. The aircraft was used by the 366th Wing whose F-111s have been replaced by F-15s, F-16s, B-1Bs and KC-135s at Mountain Home Air Force Base, Idaho.

All-black T-38A Talon 62-3699/TF307 'BB' from the 49th Fighter Wing was being prepared for departure on the AMARC ramp in October 1998. It arrived for storage in December 1995.

Above and below: Used by the Air Force as a navigation trainer, the Boeing T-43A is the military version of the Boeing 737 airliner. This aircraft, 73-1155/TH0002 'RA', has 'The Spirit of San Antonio' artwork on its nose. It arrived in September 1997 from Randolph Air Force Base, Texas, and is kept in Flyable Hold condition with minimum preservation.

Appendix One

Preserved *Desert Storm* B-52 Nose Art

57-6470	SCREAMING FOR VENGEANCE	58-0184	MISS OUACHITA II
57-6471	TANTALIZING TAKEOFF	58-0191	BEARIN' ARMS
57-6474	LONE WOLF	58-0194	BUFFASAURUS
57-6475	MIAMI CLIPPER II	58-0195	ETERNAL GUARDIAN
57-6477	A CERTAIN FURY	58-0199	SPECTRE
57-6478	STARS AND STRIPES	58-0205	WILD HARE 2
57-6483	RAGIN' CAJUN	58-0207	CITY OF MERCED
57-6485	MISS WING DING II	58-0220	NIGHT HAWK IV
57-6486	WILD THING	58-0222	TRIPLE DEUCE
57-6487	HOOSIER HOT SHOT	58-0223	SPIRIT OF AMERICA
57-6491	LITTLE PATCHES II	58-0226	WRECKIN' CREW
57-6492	OLD CROW EXPRESS	58-0229	SIOUX WARRIOR
57-6498	ACE IN THE HOLE	58-0231	HIGH ROLLER
57-6499	AGAINST THE WIND	58-0232	DISASTER MASTER
57-6501	RAGIN' RED	58-0235	
57-6502	NIGHT STALKER	58-0236	LUCKY 13
57-6503	SUPERSTITIOUS ALOISIUS	58-0238	MISS FIT II
57-6504	SNAKE EYES	58-0243	BRUTE FORCE
57-6505	DESTINATION DEVASTATION	58-0244	HELLSADROPPIN'
57-6506	COMMAND DECISION	58-0245	EQUIPOISE II
57-6508	OUTHOUSE MOUSE II	58-0249	URBAN RENEWAL
57-6509	NINE-O-NINE II	58-0250	SCREAMIN' EAGLE
57-6513	MEMPHIS BELLE II	58-0251	HONEY SUCKLE ROSE
57-6514	ROYAL FLUSH	58-0252	SAGITTARIUS II
57-6515	MOHAWK WARRIOR	58-0254	DAMAGE, INC
57-6516	ULTIMATE WARRIOR	58-0255	GUARDIAN OF PEACE
57-6518	LEO	58-0257	FIRST STRIKE
58-0162	SURPRISE ATTACK	59-2575	LARGE MARGE
58-0165	ROLLING THUNDER	59-2580	SHERIFF'S POSSE NO.2
58-0170	SPECIAL DELIVERY II	59-2581	MERVIN THE MAGICIAN
58-0171	LI'L PEACH II	59-2582	GRIM REAPER II
58-0172	THE NEGOTIATOR	59-2585	SWASHBUCKLER
58-0173	LET'S MAKE A DEAL	59-2587	STRATOFORTRESS REX
58-0175	VIPER	59-2590	BETTER DUCK II
58-0177	PETIE 3RD	59-2591	SWEET REVENGE
58-0178	OLD SOLDIER	59-2594	MEMPHIS BELLE III
58-0181	THE WITCH II	59-2598	DANGEROUS TOYS
58-0182	WHAT'S UP DOC?	59-2602	YANKEE DOODLE II
58-0183	VALKYRIE		

Appendix Two

AMARC Aircraft Inventory Comparison March 94 with October 98

Air Force

TYPE	1998	1994
A-1	2	–
A-7	25	240
A-10	189	183
A-37	3	15
B-52	116	298
B-57	12	26
YC-14	1	1
YC-15	1	1

TYPE	1998	1994
C-22	1	2
C-23	3	–
C-26	4	–
C-27	3	–
C-47	–	1
C-97	–	1
C-118	5	6
C-123	21	25
C-130	85	86
C-131	6	16

TYPE	1998	1994
C/KC-135	89	90
C-137	103	109
C-140	3	4
C-141	56	9
D-21	8	14
F-4	621	891
F-8	–	9
F-15	117	70
F-16	379	107
F-84	2	2
F-100	5	34
F-101	3	4
F-102	4	5
F-105	7	15
F-106	20	26
EF/F-111	299	198
H-1	27	32
H-3	13	20
H-53	19	19
H-54	–	1
O-2	21	68
P-2	–	2
S-2	–	1
T-29	4	4
T-33	79	104
T-37	123	89
T-38	191	157
T-39	29	27
T-43	2	–
T-46	1	2
HU-16	–	3
AV-8	–	1
OV-10	4	4
TOTAL	2,731	3,021

Navy (Including Marines)

TYPE	1998	1994
A-3	31	45
A-4	255	219
A/EA-6	200	40
A-7	236	293
C-1	19	22
C-2	5	6
C-4	7	–
C-12	7	–
C-28	2	–
C-118	1	1
C-130	3	14
C-131	12	16
E-2	23	31
F-4	201	209
F-8	18	18
F-14	107	58
F-16	12	–
F-18	55	–
H-1	59	68
H-2	47	68
H-3	72	52

TYPE	1998	1994
H-34	2	2
H-53	59	34
H-57	12	18
O-2	7	–
P-2	2	2
P-3	136	114
S-2	18	32
S-3	21	17
T-1	1	1
T-2	66	66
T-28	1	1
T-33	3	3
T-34	4	55
T-39	23	26
AV-8	38	41
OV-10	1	19
TOTAL	1,766	1,591

Army

TYPE	1998	1994
F-10	–	4
H-1	120	25
H-57	1	–
OV-1	27	31
TOTAL	148	60

Coast Guard

TYPE	1998	1994
H-3	–	36
HH-52	–	6
HU-25	15	3
TOTAL	15	45

Others   1998 only

TYPE	1998	
AV-8	1	NASA
C-22	1	Smithsonian
C-97	1	NASA (Guppy) On loan Pima Museum
C-131	2	State Department
C-137	1	Smithsonian
F-3B	2	Luftwaffe Tornadoes
OV-10	15	State Department
P-2	1	Smithsonian
P-3	1	NASA
S-2	1	Smithsonian
T-39	1	NASA

GRAND TOTAL 1998 4,687
1994 4,717